The Memory Project

A Zetz Collection

Editor: Michael Shapiro New York, New York

Design by Patrick Steven Martin New York, New York

The Memory Project

A Zetz Collection

Copyright © 2017 by Zetz Book Publishing

ISBN: 0692882774
ISBN 13: 978-0692882771
Zetz Book Publishing
New York, New York

DEDICATION

This is dedicated to anyone who has ever chased a memory and found
something they never thought they would.

CONTENTS

ACKNOWLEDGMENTS

We would like to thank Michael Shapiro and James Robinson of Columbia Journalism School and *The New York Times*, respectively, for their guidance and support as we undertook this project. We each started with only a photograph, but with their help, we pushed ourselves to create something much larger. Without Michael, we would never have discovered the *zetz*. James, were we disruptive enough?
We would also like to thank our friends and family for baring their souls to us over the course of our reporting process. Digging into these stories was revealing, bittersweet and at times painful, and we are grateful that you were willing to go through this with us.

.

PREFACE

This is what you remember.

You see the picture and the people in it or the place where it was taken and you there, just as you should remember it. But what really happened?

Memory believes, wrote William Faulkner, before knowing remembers.

Or put more prosaically: what you recall may not be what occurred.

The Memory Project is a collection of fifteen works of original narrative nonfiction built on a single, seemingly simple premise: take a photograph, a photograph you own, or see, or borrow, but a photograph that you cannot turn away from.

Consider the memory or memories triggered by that photograph. And then, when the memories come into sharp relief – the moment, the face, the encounter – stop and go back, but this time find out what lays beyond that image: what really took place? Why did someone take that photo? Why did I carry it? How did I discover it?

Who was this person I am looking at? Why can I not stop looking at him, or her? In these pages is the story about a photograph of a war photographer carried for years by a writer who never met him. There is a photograph of a ruined home in rural China where a writer's great grandfather was born and where he returned to die, alone.

There is a photograph of a child bride, a family reunion, an absent father, a gangster, a grandfather who may have killed himself, but who may not have. There is an angry woman staring at a writer as she takes her picture. A young girl on a rare happy day.

A young man captured at the moment when he is in all his glory. An uncle a writer never met but whose photograph hangs above a doorway, neither hidden nor in plain sight.

1

The best stories, the stories we need to read, the stories we discover and cannot put down and cannot wait to tell others about, are the stories that transport us.

Be they works of imagination or journalism they share a common trait: they are stories a writer needed to tell. We know it because when we read it we feel it.

Welcome to The Memory Project.

"Memory believes before knowing remembers."
–William Faulkner

1 THAT YOUNG MAN

He was happy in an unhappy nation in an unhappy time. He lived to fight.

By Tori Otten

H e is perfect. That's what everyone says when I show them this picture. He is young, and beautiful and at his physical peak. He can also be vicious. "I beat up so many guys," he would later tell me. "Maybe one, two a day."

"Has that photo always been there?" I asked my aunt one day when I was visiting.

"Oh, yes," she replied.

I'd visited my Aunt Ock Nam's apartment before. She and my uncle lived on the outskirts of Vienna but kept an apartment in town. I was studying abroad, and visiting for fall break. Ock Nam went into the kitchen to grab a few things, and I walked into the living room. A black and white photograph, hanging in the corner, caught my eye.

I had been in this apartment many times before, but I never remembered seeing this photo. From behind the glass, a young Asian man stared back at me. He was more ripped and defined than I thought a human being could be.

"I never remember seeing it before," I said.

"Well," she replied, "it's always been there."

"Who is *that?*" I asked.

"That's Grandpa," she said.

"That's *Grandpa?*" I asked, picturing the small, increasingly frail old man I'd always known.

"Yes," she said. "That's when he was about your age. He wanted to be a boxer."

This photo is an ice sculpture. Inevitably, it will melt.

Japan invaded Korea in 1910, when the north and south were still a unified nation. For centuries before then, Korea had been the Hermit Kingdom. Isolated from the rest of the world, the country promoted its own culture, its own language, and its own accomplishments. Korea enjoyed peace and stability for over 200 years. Korea had often referred to itself as "a shrimp among whales" – a small country subject to the whims and conflicts of the powers around it – Japan and China. When the Japanese arrived, Korea didn't stand a chance.

The Japanese ruled Korea for 30 brutal years. Korea no longer existed. *Hangul*, Korea's alphabet, was banned. Children spoke Japanese in school and went by Japanese names. Scholars were publicly humiliated for their Korean traditions, and people were made to worship at Shinto shrines. Anything made of metal, such as hairpins, jewelry, or even fancy chopsticks and plates, had to be given to the military to be melted down and made into weapons. People were forced to provide resources for the soldiers, and young women were shipped to the front lines to serve as prostitutes for the Japanese soldiers.

My grandfather grew up in this world.

He was born in 1938 in Munsan, a village in the middle of the country on the south bank of the Imjin River. When he was two years old, his mother died. He never found out why. But he does remember, as a young boy, running around his home asking where his mother was. No one would tell him.

His father eventually remarried, but the new wife, my mother told me, didn't want my grandfather. She refused to feed him and his older brother, even though the family had enough money to take care of everyone. My grandfather would go to his uncle's house to get fed, and he ended up living with his grandparents.

And then, one day, Korea woke up to find the Japanese gone.

As World War II drew to a close, the Allies agreed to support Korean independence but ended up splitting the country in half. The Americans controlled the south. In the north, the Soviets installed a puppet regime. With the Japanese gone, Korea descended into five years of political turmoil. The two Koreas were recognized as separate nations, and the U.S. withdrew from Korea by 1949.

War broke out almost immediately. Where South Korea had no military, North Korea had spent the previous five years undergoing extensive military development. The South was unprepared in 1950 when the North crossed the 38th Parallel, quickly taking Seoul, the southern capitol, and obliterating the South Korean armed forces.

My grandfather was 12.

The war dragged on with attack followed by counterattack, culminating in a stalemate in 1953. The 38th Parallel became the border between the two Koreas. Military forces on both sides pulled back 1.2 miles from the Parallel, creating the De-Militarized Zone. No peace treaty was signed. The two countries would remain technically at war.

It was around this time that my grandfather started getting into fights. The decades of occupation and tenuous peace and all-out war had left Korea devastated. People were starving to death. Mothers would abandon their infants by the side of the road, unable to care for them.

"That's war," my grandfather told me. "You've got no country. Your country has to be strong. You have to be strong."

He started running errands for the American military. And he started getting into fights almost every day. If he didn't fight, he wouldn't eat.

"There were gangsters all over the place," he said. "Sometimes they beat me up. Sometimes I beat them up. If you wanted something, you had to fight and take it."

The American soldiers introduced him to boxing. Seeing the fights sparked something in him – he knew what he wanted to become. When I asked him why he wanted to be a boxer, he gave me an unsatisfying answer. "I wanted to stand out," he said. "When you're from a foreign country, you have to have something special."

But boxing isn't special. It's the simplest thing in the world. You hit and you kick and you fight until someone starts to bleed.

I could not reconcile that concept with the quiet, mild-mannered man I had always known as my grandfather. Why would he want to fight?

My grandfather is not a talkative man, and getting him to speak of the past, and especially motives for his behavior, is impossible.

So to understand why he might have found a certain pleasure in fighting, I sought out boxers, who might be able to explain my grandfather to me.

I went to Gleason's, a legendary fight gym in Brooklyn. I began by showing the fighters and their trainers the photo. They were impressed. They wanted to know how he did in the ring. I told them that his career was limited mostly to street fighting.

Why, I asked, does anyone fight? Most of their answers were, like my grandfather's, anodyne, safe. But Eric Kelly, a national champion as an amateur, who later fought professionally and who now trains fighters, told me something illuminating.

"I fight because I'm violent," he said. "The fight is in me. I'm dangerous." He moved to Brooklyn in the 80s to live with his dad, and he got in fights every day at school or in his neighborhood. His dad sent him to the boxing gym. Eric stopped fighting only because he got so badly injured during a fight that he lost muscle control in half of his face.

"Everyone in here is crazy," he said. "Why else would you want to hit somebody in the face and get hit in the face back?"

The Koreans have a word to describe an emotion that they feel is theirs alone: *Han*. It translates roughly as unresolvable bitterness. My grandfather came of age without a country, without a family, and without prospects. He was hungry and he was angry and he liked to hit people.

But for reasons he does not explain, he did not see a future in the ring. Instead, even while working for the American military, he stayed in school. Still, when he was 19, just finishing up high school, he and a friend got ahold of a camera. My grandfather, young and chiseled and glorious, posed for a few photos.

"That picture of me, all naked on top?" he said when I asked him about the photo. He laughed. "It was just for fun." That was 1956.

My grandfather went on to get a degree in engineering. Two years later, when he was 21, he married my grandmother. They had four daughters, and he continued to work for the American military. He could make money and also have access to the military PX (the army's version of Walmart).

"We always had strawberry jam," my mother told me. "And a TV. Sometimes we didn't even have electricity, but we had a TV."

In 1963, Park Chung-Hee seized power of South Korea in a military coup. In 1971, my grandparents moved their family to the United States and resettled in northern Virginia. They lived with distant cousins for a little while, while my grandfather worked to save up enough money to get their own home. The only work he could find was in construction.

At the second construction company where he worked, the owner took a liking to him and offered to mentor his rise in the company. But my grandfather instead asked if his boss would help him start his own company. The boss agreed.

My grandfather worked 18-hour days. He rarely saw his daughters, but still he quizzed them on multiplication tables every morning. When my aunt Christi was in fourth grade, she got in trouble at school for punching a girl who had been bullying her.

"I was just doing what Grandpa always said," Christi told me. "It's better to hit first than to be hit."

My grandfather had succeeded in all ways but one: his marriage fell apart.

My grandfather always told his children that the one thing he could never forgive was someone leaving his wife. So when he and my grandmother started to have trouble, he insisted on staying. It did not last. In 1994, my aunt Ock Nam was preparing to move to

Vienna with her husband. My grandparents were living separately. In the basement of my grandmother's house, Ock Nam found the photograph of my grandfather as a young man and took it with her. Two years later, my grandmother asked for a divorce.

Ock Nam was always the closest to my grandfather. She went to college at Virginia Tech, just a few hours away from home. She came home almost every weekend. She lives in Vienna, but she spends every free vacation trip she has coming back home, where she insists that she, her husband, and their daughter stay at my grandma's house, sleeping in the same bedroom she slept in while growing up.

My grandfather was her ideal man. When he agreed to leave, he wasn't just leaving the family, or her mother. He left her.

"She couldn't forgive her human father," my mom told me. "She only remembers her perfect father."

The walls of my aunt's apartment are covered with photos – full color shots of the sisters with their boyfriends (now husbands), pictures of my grandma, new glossy photos of the kids. They're all clustered together, without boundaries and almost uncomfortably close, just like the relationships within my family.

The photo of my grandfather hangs alone, in a corner, obscured by a lamp.

My grandfather is 79. He never remarried. He and my grandmother don't speak with each other unless they have to.

He doesn't remember the first person he beat up. He doesn't remember how many fights he got into. He says he got married in part because it forced him to get a job and kept him out of jail.

He loves his grandchildren, and we love him back, but we don't see him that often. He's still always working. He doesn't talk about himself. He asks how I'm doing, what I'm doing, if I'm making friends and getting good grades. He wants to know if I'm happy.

I am not much older than he is in that picture, where he was captured in a rare moment of joy.

But that was after everything that came before, and before everything that came after.

\- - -

TORI OTTEN *is a writer who focuses on long-form narrative journalism and fiction. You can find her other work at medium.com/@teotten*

POSTSCRIPT

As I mentioned in my story, I saw this photo three years ago, and it's been on my mind ever since. When I first decided to report this photo, I didn't even know what question I was trying to answer for myself. I just knew that I had to write about this photo.

I started by talking to my grandpa, trying to understand why he wanted to be a boxer. I also talked to my mom, asking her the same thing. As it turned out, the story wasn't about why he wanted to be a boxer. It always came back to the photo.

I started to research Korea, both under Japanese occupation and after the Korean War, to try and understand the world in which my grandfather grew up. Then, I started interviewing boxing coaches, all of whom were former boxers. I asked them why they fought, and things started to become clear.

I went back to my grandpa, and my mom, and my aunt. I needed to understand everything about that photo - why it was taken, how it ended up in Vienna. The more I found out, the more I kept returning to the photo - what it represented about the past and the future to everyone who came into contact with it.

2 DOJO RATS

Running a karate school is hard, but it's harder when it's your family.

By Patrick Martin

My parents ran a nice business when I was a kid. They both had corporate careers in Memphis, but when the workday ended they met at the karate school they ran. They changed into their uniforms. My dad would start to teach, and my mom recruited new students. They loved it, and I did, too.

There were two other teachers, Joe and David, and my parents treated them like family. That's what made what happened so much harder.

It all started because I loved the Ninja Turtles. I must have been about six. I had plastic-framed Coke bottle glasses. The Ninja Turtles were huge at the time, and I was obsessed. I dragged all my big sister's boyfriends into my room to show them my Playmates Teenage Mutant Ninja Turtles Playset Sewer Lair. It had the green plastic tube connectors to transform the sewer into a world full of Shredder, the turtles and Domino's pizza.

I wanted to be just like the turtles, so my mom took me for karate lessons. The school was run by a man named Michael who was a third-degree black belt with longer wiry hair and a bald spot in the middle. He was short in his mid-40s. He told everyone he opened the school because he was mugged and never wanted to be a victim again.

My dad would bring me when he got off work. He would sit in the uncomfortable folding chairs and just watch. He could have balanced his checkbook or caught up on work, but he just watched us punch and kick. "Dad got such a kick out of you in the little dragons that I bought him lessons for Valentine's Day," my mom, Stephanie, told me. My father, Frank, returned the favor, getting her lessons for Mother's Day.

Soon we were all into it, except for my older sister, who couldn't be bothered. Later we adopted the motto: "A family that kicks together sticks together."

The school had been a video store before being transformed into a martial arts studio. It was connected to a Big Star grocery store—part of a popular mid-south supermarket chain. It had two training floors surrounded by mirrors and a viewer's section where parents and friends could watch. The school's original colors were purple, sea foam green, peach and white. Picture the Batman villain the Joker, in the animated series—same color pallette. The studio looked like a rejected set for Miami Vice.

The more involved my parents got with the school, the more they started to see that Michael wasn't a good fit for running it. He was bad with money–bills were unpaid. There were growing tensions between him and one of the other instructors. Finally, one day he was gone. "He was a legend in his own damn mind," my mom said. "The bottom line is he was out."

Which meant that, soon after, my parents were in.

The school was now Joe Wilson's. Joe was 18, straight out of high school. He'd done karate since he was 4 years old. Joe loved the martial arts. His morning breakfast was a bowl of cereal with a side of flying side kick. He looked like a martial artist. Joe could do a 12 o'clock kick to the ceiling with ease. He always wore a black bandana. The other teacher, David Curry, was in his early 20s and on the hefty side. He had blond hair parted to the side with almost feathered bangs—it was a typical haircut in Memphis at the time—and a pillow-like mid-section. Whenever he would do any stretches or raise his arms, his gi—his uniform top—would become untucked. Not to say David wasn't athletic.

"It's surprising to see someone that big who could move so fluidly," Joe said about David.

The school was now Joe's.

"The school was officially mine, but I really didn't know what I was doing," he told me. "I was a kid, and I was teaching. Other than that, I really didn't know anything about bank accounts."

He decided to hire David to help run it. "He pitched me," Joe said about David: "Look, I have a business degree, and I can help."

My parents also offered to volunteer more of their time. They even offered to sign the lease and never asked for a penny of profit. The property company and my parents negotiated an agreement where my parents wouldn't have to pay the past due amount. The first thing all four of the partners did was change the name of the school. We were now the Memphis Martial Arts Academy.

We re-painted the school to look more like a traditional dojo compared to a totally tubular 80's hangout like you would see in those cheesy snowboarding movies.

"I wanted to cleanse the school," Joe said of his predecessor. "He was a weird dude."

By this time my mother was managing all the programs the school had, and was officially listed as Program Director. My dad advised the partners and taught—he enjoyed the workouts and losing 30 pounds: "I loved to go in there to do the training and get my belly off." They had all attended a conference in Orlando on the business of running a karate school. They learned about billing, attendance, expansion and recruiting. They learned that it was imperative that they sell themselves with the words, "We are a black belt school."

My mom is incredibly organized and saved all her program material. There were tabs for everything—breathing patterns, kicks, punches, forms, to say nothing of all the administrative material. The school was designed to lead each student from white belt all the way to black, with the colors getting ever darker at each stage. It could take years.

My parents' lives revolved around running the school and work. They both had jobs with a lot of responsibility outside of the martial arts. My father was a senior branch manager at Commercial Credit Financial Services with more than 10 people under him. My mother was a vice president at a Memphis stock brokerage firm—Carty and Company.

Every day you would see my parents and the instructors on the floor training students. My mom would teach a class here and there, but she was more worried about signing up new students. The school had a system. It was all about promoting karate as a product. Something anybody could do.

It started by memorizing the student creed to get your white belt. It was the first belt in a system of 10. In my mom's program manual, there is a whole section on how to award students. The point was to keep them wanting more. As a student progressed through the belt system, new options would open as you advanced in rank.

We had the Black Belt Club, and the coveted S.W.A.T or Special Winning Attitude Team. S.W.A.T. members could be assistant instructors and got special red uniform tops. S.W.A.T. was one of the biggest goals for any student, topped only by getting a black belt. The Memphis Martial Arts Academy knew how to award those who stuck with it till the end. The academy would have a black belt spectacular—a bacchanal of all things karate in a 90-minute show for friends and family, followed by a reception. The prize was a black belt with the person's name embroidered at the end with red letters.

"We did demonstrations, we had video, we had fog machines," my dad said. "And remember, we supplied the belt."

My parents and I became candidates for black belts. This meant having to endure a weekend filled with high-stress testing called "Power Weekend," when the school reeked of sweaty vinyl and foam from the sparring gear. My parents were already black belts when my turn came and I remember sparring with my mom. They had taken things more seriously than I had.

"Keep your guard up!" my mom hollered at me as she delivered a front kick right to the face. A teaching moment that left me with a bloody nose.

"You ran into my foot," my mom now says. "I will believe that until the day I die."

E ach week the four business partners would have team meetings. My mom and dad kept minutes of every meeting with a running log of action items that needed to be accomplished during the week.

"To me these were necessary," my dad said. "We had to keep the staff advised of what was going on."

"Staff Meeting 1/11/96

Need to develop flyer for Grand Opening (late February)
Sam (my mom's nickname) checking with Mary Robinson about getting new letter for front sign. Need to find out about panels on 'street' sign"

They even sold the old merchandise with the old logo as collectors' items.

David and Joe called my parents mom and dad. They would come over every Sunday for dinner. I remember Joe always being the most excited when my mom made an Italian dish Braciole—hammered flank steak rolled with mushrooms, cheese and ham on the inside.

I thought it was a traditional Sunday dinner with family. But, I've since learned that these dinners were also board meetings. Joe was more of the curriculum guy, while David would try to be the marketing guy—a lot of flyers with pull off tabs. My dad would oversee all operations and lend his voice during disputes.

At its height, the Memphis Martial Arts Academy had 150 students each paying $75 a month. With the sale of merchandise, shirts for the hugely popular tee-shirt night, sparring gear and special weekend self-defense seminars at $99 a person, the school made about $20,000 a month.

Still, my dad told me, "we barely broke even every month. It was tough, but we were growing."

Everyone wanted to see the school grow. My parents thought the best way would be to expand the student base. David had another idea. Invest in an expensive low-budget commercial, selling the academy with David as the spokesperson. Picture a used car commercial with sweeping shots of the car lot followed by a talking head advertising low prices that can't be beat. That's what the karate school commercial would have looked like.

The karate school had already done a commercial a few years back. The fondest memory Joe had of the old commercial was almost coughing up a lung while not being able to see anything.

"The commercial itself, I remember a voiceover and smoke; I remember doing a jump spin kick in smoke," Joe said. "It wasn't even a smoke machine. It was this smoke pot they lit, probably a base form of CS"—tear gas.

Looking through the meeting minutes, you can see David and Joe starting to pursue more aggressive advertising. "David will check Papa Johns for box toppers." And "David and Joe have a preliminary meeting with WLMT for back to school promotions."

My parents were not so sure. "You had to see it from our side," my dad said. "Why would we make a commercial with money we didn't have?"

The commercial was estimated at $10,000, not including studio time. Plus, David was more concerned about getting new students then retaining old ones. The team put together a plan called 2-4-6 calls. Here's how it worked: David was supposed to call students two weeks after a student quit coming to classes, four weeks and finally six weeks. He didn't do it.

Instead, David was more worried that my parents had too much involvement in the school. He was worried that Joe was getting paid more. He was worried that he wasn't making money.

On June 15, 1997, the minutes show that both David and Joe would make the same salary, $18,100 a year, until revenues improved where both subsequent salaries would increase at the same rate.

In late June, my parents got a call one night. I remember it being about 9 p.m. The sky felt darker that day. It was a maintenance guy at the school who was doing some overnight work. He said his key didn't work.

My parents jumped in the car with me in tow to figure out what was wrong. Both my mom and dad forgot if they called David or Joe. They just remember driving to the school.

There were three doors, a main entrance, side entrance and back alley entrance. We tried the main entrance. My dad put the key in, but nothing happened. The key passed through all the tumblers, but he couldn't turn it.

We were locked out. David had changed the locks earlier in the day after my parents left.

The three of us were looking through the windows at the school we thought was our home, only to realize things would never be the same.

"They were great memories we had at the school," my dad now says. "I mean yeah, some other stuff went on, but we just look past that. I devoted my friggin' life to that school."

Joe Wilson still has great affection for my parents. "Your parents were above and beyond very good to me, " he told me. "They treated me like their child."

Even after they'd been locked out, my parents still came to class, even though things did not feel the same.

"When I think about your parents, I don't remember the locks thing," Joe said, "but I just remember being sad."

The school slowly started to falter. Students left and profits plummeted. With my family not as firmly invested, we had an excuse to move. We moved into my late grandma's house in south Florida when I was in seventh grade.

Joe went into debt keeping the school open until he became a cop at 21. I learned that the hard way. Had things gone differently, it probably would have been an easier education, he said.

I spoke to my mom about the times at the school and how uneasy Joe was after everything went down, how Joe wasn't on board with what David did. I told her about how he spent weeks and weeks just feeling "weird" after everything that happened.

Her reply: "Good. If it wasn't for that night, we probably would still be in Memphis at the school."

- - -

PATRICK MARTIN is a writer and Army veteran who has written everything from business, crime to everything in-between.. You can find his other work at medium.com/@patrick_martin

POSTSCRIPT

I could have chosen a thousand pictures. Everyone I spoke to thought it was an interesting story but asked me why not one of my military stories. Why don't I do a picture on the literally 100s of pictures I have from the wars. Michael Shapiro put it into the easiest terms, and I agree with him. The story needed to be told now.

My time at the karate school was one of the great memories I have from Memphis. But, I put all the evil grown up things that happened in the shadows in the back of my head. The reporting and original angle was about a rite of passage I had with Joe as my mentor. I was hiding from the real story. It was time to shine the light into the shadows. I needed to find out why my parents were locked out. I needed to know who was the villain, who was the hero?

Once I knew what the angle was, I talked to my parents. It was a strange sensation interviewing my parents. You'd think I could ask them anything, but they were just like any other source. They hid information or were vague in some of the answers. Thankfully, my mom kept records of EVERYTHING. She sent me a three-ring binder with any and everything I needed to ask about the karate school. I had meeting minutes, advertising strategy, regulations for promotions and how the school would progress in the next few years.

My next stop was to interview Joe. He was hazy on the memories, but it was the first time I heard the story from every angle. One recommendation I would have when reporting on a memoir like this is to be open to new lines of reporting that become available. I had no idea how deep the story went. I still think there is more I can find out. You never know, maybe this is a start to a bigger story, perhaps a book.

3 SEVENTEEN FOREVER

I never knew my uncle. I didn't know I could ask

By E.K. Hudson

This is how I met my uncle: It was summer. We were at our cottage in Milford Bay, two hours north of Toronto. I was maybe eight years old and I think we were eating dinner.

"Have we ever had a cat instead of a dog?" I remember asking my mom. She told me yes; her family used to have a cat named Buttons and she had a picture. She took a chair and stood on it to reach a photo that had been hanging above the dining room doorway. She took down this photo: half of Buttons is sitting on the couch beside a teenage boy with long skater hair and broad shoulders.

The boy isn't smiling, but doesn't seem angry either. His face looks familiar somehow. The couch and faux wood paneling behind him don't look like our house or my grandparents'.

"Who's that?" I asked. Adults I didn't know intimidated me, particularly men and boys. I didn't grow up seeing our extended family, mostly boys, often and my immediate family was mostly women, so what was this boy doing in a framed photo hanging on the wall of our cottage?

"It's your Uncle Stephen."

I knew my mom had a younger brother, but I'd never knowingly seen him before that moment. Suddenly, it made sense why I recognized his eyes and brows – it's my mom's gaze. I think I understood intuitively not to ask another question, not because my mom, Lynn, and my grandparents, Norman and Marion, wouldn't answer, but because there was no point. He was gone, nothing would change that, and, in my family, we cry or we stay silent – there's seldom any ground between the two. We have a saying in our family: It's not a lively family discussion unless someone cries. So, Stephen stayed on the wall like a window into another time, which we knew of, but not about, until years later.

***

The first thing I learned when I decided to get to know the boy in the picture was that everyone called him Steve. Steve was my mom's little brother by about two years – the same age difference between me and my little sister.

He was 17 when, in January 1978, he went skiing with his friends. My grandparents told him to stay home and do his math homework – he wasn't a good student and university applications were looming. A snowstorm was forecast and roads would be bad. But Steve was at his best in motion, so he went.

On the way home, he sat next to the driver. Steve's best friend Peter Kuntz sat in the back. As the car drove out of the ski hill's parking lot, it hit a patch of black ice. They swung into oncoming traffic and collided with a pickup truck. There was one fatality.

Almost two hundred people showed up to Steve's funeral. Someone played Stevie Wonder's *A Place in the Sun* on the guitar. Afterwards at the reception, Steve's friends sat in the basement of my grandparent's house in stunned silence.

My mom Lynn went back to university and her friends kept their distance. What do you say to someone who lost her brother? She was now a living reminder of something no one wanted to think about.

Norman, her father, rarely spoke about his son for years afterwards. He blamed himself. He knew the storm was getting worse; he should have called them that day and told them to spend the night in a nearby hotel.

Her mother Marion had to reconcile the rascal her son was at 17 with the man she'd been hoping he'd become. But all she had left was this photo – an imperfect moment from a less than ideal time in their family.

***

Almost 40 years later, the first memories that came to Marion's 91-year-old mind when I asked about Steve included the time he abandoned her in a sailboat in the middle of a lake, the time he tipped over their snowmobile pinning her underneath and finally, the time she found marijuana hidden in his room.

"He had no patience," she said. Each time he'd stranded her, either on water or waist-deep in snow, she didn't lecture him. "What's the point?" she told me with a strained smile and forced laugh as she cleaned breakfast dishes. Exasperating my grandma Marion, the perpetual optimist, to the point of resigned acceptance is a notable feat Steve seemed to have mastered over his high school years.

Left home alone one weekend, Steve hosted a party that had to be broken up by the neighbors. He and a friend threw bottle caps into the same neighbor's pool as part of a game. He didn't do well in school and, when he went out on weekends, he would never call to tell his parents where he was.

One night, Marion waited up for him until 2 a.m. with no clue of where her son might be. When he finally ambled in, Marion was furious. Her response to the boy who never seemed to listen was visceral: "I swatted him on the backside. I was so upset."

Marion, at 5 foot 6 inches tall, was a tough but slender woman. Steve, who was "probably 16" at the time, towered over his mother. The idea of Marion hitting him is laughable, but she was frustrated enough to try anyway. Steve apologized and explained why he was so late: he'd missed the bus and walked for hours to get home.

It would happen again and again. Steve and his friends would disappear – sometimes to listen to a band play nearby – but the point was he never asked, so Marion and Norman wouldn't know where he'd gone. "Bad things happen to boys too," she told me. "It's not just girls."

***

Lynn remembered her parents and Steve fighting over everything. Norman and Marion tried to recruit Lynn to help their efforts, asking her to speak with Steve, but she didn't want to get involved; this was between them. Besides, she didn't think he was doing anything really wrong.

She told me that Steve was a favorite crush among the girls at Erindale Secondary School, though he never had a girlfriend. He played hockey until he was 15 and then decided to quit; he wasn't going to the NHL—only the coaches' sons would get that opportunity—so he decided it was time to try something new.

Every Sunday, he would drive or take the bus into the east end of Toronto to go to skateboard. In school, Steve focused on track and field. He ran and specialized in pole vaulting; he liked the idea of going up and over the high bar. Like Lynn, he worked part time after school at a golf club and a shipping depot. He was always on time. When my grandparents decided to renovate the family cottage, Steve and Lynn were put to work – building the porch, shingling, painting, gardening and mowing the lawn.

My mother and her brother were close, rivals but best friends. Though they ran in different circles, Lynn started introducing Steve to some of her friends. She was part of the right crowd and Steve seemed to like her friends. So, before she graduated from Erindale in spring of 1976 and moved an hour away to university, there was hope.

***

Months later when Lynn was home for the holidays, she would take the photo that would become how Steve was remembered. It seemed like it would be a nice photo to have of that Christmas.

The moment Lynn captured excludes any details that would indicate the season or that my grandparents were around. She did it on purpose; she didn't want any forced smiles in the picture. She wanted a real photo that could pass as part of a nice Christmas, even if just for a moment. For the illusion to be possible, she couldn't let her mom or dad in the photo and risk shattering what she saw through the viewfinder: Steve looking happy.

"I just thought it was a really great photo," she told me.

But things at home were strained. Six months earlier, while cleaning Steve's room, my grandma Marion found the marijuana. She and Norman were furious, though Lynn remembered Marion being the most vocal. They told Steve in no uncertain terms that doing drugs was grounds for eviction in the Goodayle household. If he wanted to continue getting high, he would have to find a new place to live.

Lynn was horrified at their reaction. She and her friends would drink beer despite being under-aged, often at the cottage with her parent's supervision. They'd established ground rules: no driving; no boating. But pot was different. It was a drug, not a coming-of-age beverage. And Steve would never consult his parents.

Lynn didn't think Steve had a "significant problem" and, considering his group of friends, she wasn't surprised he was smoking. He was working part-time at a truck depot – "trucking and drugs are pretty notorious" – and Lynn didn't think that environment was a permanent place for Steve. It was just one phase in the life of her brother.

Marion, a devout Christian and working mother, saw it differently. She'd grown in up in the small town of Vernon, B.C. in Western Canada where a local youth group and her large extended family served as her gateway into the world. Youth to my grandma meant helping with farm work on her grandfather's ranch, listening to her aunts tell scandalous jokes and stories, and, when World War Two started, going to army dances with her brother as her date. Marion knew how to have fun, but she did so following the rules.

Knowing this, the idea that using drugs warranted kicking her son out of the house does not surprise me. Never one to hold back her opinions, I remember feeling grumpy one day when I was maybe 11 and her saying, "Gee, I hope this doesn't reflect how Erin will turn out."

So, that Christmas, the tension between my grandparents and Steve was palpable, so much so that my mom isolated Steve in this photo to try and save a happy memory from it.

***

The truth of whether Steve was throwing away his life or on the cusp of growing up is somewhere in between.

Peter Kuntz, one of Steve's friends, visits his grave every so often – a place I've never been. "He was my best buddy," he told me. Peter is 56 and the father of two.

They met in Grade 9 and were "chumming around" until the accident. They would go to Steve's place for lunch and listen to Deep Purple, Pink Floyd and Supertramp on Steve's Marantz stereo receiver.

They'd goof around in the big yard and Peter would stick around even when Steve had chores to do.

At the cottage, they'd tie a rope to the boat Steve was allowed to drive, grab a plywood board and drag each other across the bay. Steve was the only friend Peter spent so much time with and the constant backdrop to everything they did was smoking pot. "There was a stretch there," he said, "where we were high every day."

"I remember being in English class, and we'd toke up before going in," he said. Getting high was just for "shits and giggles," but Peter got serious the next year and got into university.

"I imagine Steve would have done the same," he said.

Norman and Marion couldn't believe that—every teacher confirmed their son was a poor student, except for one, Steve's grade 12 architectural drafting teacher, Christopher Parr. He thought Steve was a mature, introspective young man. Parr attended the funeral and sent a letter a week later with Steve's final exam attached. The exam was a mock questionnaire for applicants to the University of Toronto's architecture school, one of the country's top institutions in the field. "You demonstrate sufficient depth of thought that would grant you a continued interview. In other words – you pass!" Parr wrote in red pen on Steve's exam.

The closest I'll ever get to knowing what Steve thought is a series of essays he wrote in grade 12 English. Lynn found them in his locker two hours before his funeral. He wrote in looping cursive about his feelings on good and evil, his family and Christmas. He wrote about being shy, how German Shepherds personified evil and explained why he believed in God, even though most of friends didn't. He wrote about being teased for his crooked front tooth – "people can be cruel" – and how he came home crying from high school one day. He appreciated how his mom reacted: she made an appointment to get him braces.

He also wrote about his older sister helping him feel comfortable around new people when he started high school and how his dad always stood by the finish line, yelling loudly, at his track races.

"No matter what barrier I have to overcome in my life, I know that my parents and sister will be there to help me and I will be around to help them over big obstacles," he wrote in November 1977, about two months before his family would face their biggest obstacle.

Three days before he died, he turned in his Christmas essay. It was the best time of the year because "it's the only time of the year when people seem to be happy and nice to one another."

***

If you flip through Steve's photo album, which was put together by his mother, it's clear high school changed him. The first few pages are filled with big smiles and action. There are photos of him balancing on top of his highchair, sitting on a tipping chair and perching on a rocking horse standing on tiptoes. At 14, his transformation from a wide grin to a closed-mouth stare begins.

In his grade 9 school photo his blond hair covers his ears. He's wearing a cotton plaid shirt and looks like a grinning troublemaker. The next photo shows him on initiation day, wearing short shorts and a white halter top that exposes 4 inches of his abdomen. He's smiling as if to say, "here we go." A year later, his chin-length hair looks electrically charged as it fans out around his ears. He's smiling with eyes half shut, as though in a happy daze. In grade 11, he stares blankly, his mouth in a straight line, tolerating the camera. His hair is cut into a styled man-bob with bangs and layers. There's no grade 12 picture.

The last photo in the album is one I've never seen before: Steve is sitting on a chairlift, his back ramrod straight as he holds his skis and poles neatly. Marion's handwritten caption read: "Wonderful day skiing." It's dated January 20, 1978. The next page shows a two-inch by two-inch square newspaper clipping – the obituary. The rest of the album is blank.

***

Friday January 20, 1978 was a gorgeous day, but the weather forecast promised otherwise. Norman and Marion had made a deal with Steve the night before: if the weather was bad, he would stay home. If the sun came up, he would go. Marion saw him off. "Goodbye, have fun and be careful," she told him. He got into his friend's compact car and they were off.

The trip was Peter's idea. He and two friends Steve didn't know too well were going skiing. Steve wasn't a serious skier – he didn't own skis like the other boys, but that didn't stop him from doing tricks off the mountain's jumps. At the end of the day, getting ready for the two-hour drive home, Steve and Peter both wanted the prime seat – the front seat.

Peter remembered a coin toss. Steve called heads and Queen Elizabeth II's bust landed face up; Peter was relegated to the back seat, sitting directly behind the driver, Andrew Scheve. The trip ended up being a short one.

The accident happened at 5:55 p.m., in the west end of Collingwood, a short distance from the ski hill. Peter remembered going over a bridge when they hit black ice and spun out. Andrew got them straightened out, but the wheels were still facing the wrong direction, the front-wheel drive propelling them into oncoming traffic. Then the pick-up truck slammed into the right side of their car. The windshield shattered, cutting the boys' skin. Blood coated the dash and the inside of the car. Andrew's body smacked into the steering wheel, rupturing his spleen. In the front seat, Steve sat still, slumped forward with his chin resting on his chest, gurgling.

It's unclear how long it took for the ambulance to arrive. The two men who'd been driving the pick-up truck left the scene. Peter remembered the smell of beer. Allegedly, they'd had an open case of beer and returned to the accident only after drinking coffee in a nearby café. When the paramedics arrived, Peter, who emerged relatively unscathed, rode in the ambulance with Steve. He was still breathing.

By the time they arrived at Collingwood's General and Marine Hospital and rolled Steve into the hospital, it was over. Peter, watching from the side, went into a state of shock. He doesn't remember anything more from that night, but Lynn heard that he'd walked out of the hospital after hearing Steve was dead and nearly got hit by a car. The hospital staff brought Peter back inside, gave him Steve's gold watch. Peter doesn't remember a watch. Then they sedated him. His first memory after the accident was waking up on Saturday morning with his step-mom Trudy standing beside his hospital bed.

***

Two hours away, around 6:30 p.m., the phone rang. "Hello?" said Norman. It was someone calling from the Collingwood hospital with some questions: Do you have a son and does he wear braces?

"Yes?" Norman stood in the back hallway of the house, fielding the questions. It was early evening and they'd already eaten supper. He listened as the caller explained there'd been an accident: his son was dead.

The first thing Norman did was tell Marion. Then they called the minister of their church, Tim Foley. He came over right away and suggested a prayer. They kneeled together in the living room and, as Marion prayed next to couch, she knew who was with her. "I just had a sense that God was right there. I just knew He was," she said. After that, the decisions came easily.

There were no tears. They called Lynn at university and arranged her ride home. The next day, Saturday, Norman went to Collingwood to identify Steve's body. Then he and Marion went to the funeral home to choose a casket; the funeral would be held on Monday. The minister insisted on coming with them – he'd seen too many grieving families get talked into buying an expensive casket, but he needn't have worried about the Goodayles. "We had our feet on the ground," Marion told me.

"How is that possible?" I asked her.

"I don't know if I can explain it to you," she replied.

***

In school on Monday, the hallways were buzzing with the news: a student died over the weekend. It wasn't the first or last time history teacher George Brett would learn of a student's death like this, but what made this time notable was the family. It was the Goodayle family's son.

George's first thoughts went to Steve's parents, Marion and Norman Goodayle, whom George still remembered from parents' night in fall 1975, two years before. He taught Steve history that year. George remembered the Goodayles because they'd remembered him. His family had lived down the road from the couple on the Fifth Line. George had only been six at the time, so he had few memories of them, but Marion regaled him with stories that parents' night. He'd been charmed, but not enough to alter the facts about their son's lazy performance in his class.

Giving his sympathies to Norman and Marion that afternoon at the funeral, George was surprised and touched when Marion invited him back to the house for a reception for close friends. He went and that's when he got a lesson on who his former student had really been. Marion told George about the marijuana and the trouble Steve gave them.

"Well, how many kids at that school *didn't* have marijuana in their bedrooms?" George thought, but he was surprised. It wasn't what he expected from Steve Goodayle, the son of a church-going family. George stayed in touch with the grieving Goodayles. He acted like a big brother for Lynn, taking her phone calls, visiting her at university, and he checked in on Marion and Norman. He liked and admired them.

"It's not uncommon for the death of a child to tear the family apart and it didn't tear your family apart," he told me. "I've always been very much an admirer of the way your grandparents have dealt with it."

***

"Dealing with it" meant dealing with God. It meant making peace with God's purpose for Steve – this was how Marion explained it to me in 2016. "God was leading him into this," she said, handing me a box of Kleenex. A story like Steve giving a friend's mother an unexpected hug the last time she saw him became packed with symbolic meaning for my grandma. Once she saw it as part of God's plan, his death qualified as "wonderful" and "beautiful."

"He didn't suffer," she told me. "He was killed instantly."

"He was what?" My grandpa Norman had been listening from across the apartment. He can't hear well and dementia wreaks havoc on his memory, but he recognized Steve's name.

"He was killed instantly," Marion repeated louder with force. It took her 40 years to arrive at this understanding.

My mom Lynn told me later Marion once knew the truth—that Steve was alive for some time in the crashed car—but at some point she chose to forget. For Lynn, it's a choice she can't make: one memory in particular is seared into her mind.

It was spring 1978 and the smooth alto voice of Linda Ronstadt was ricocheting through their small house. Lyrics about heartbreak, punctuated by pulsing guitar and piano, blasted contradictory messages of a woman on the mend yet simultaneously drowning in loneliness. It was a fitting soundtrack for a post-breakup bender, not so much for a mother mourning her son. But Marion and Linda didn't care what anyone else thought – they'd taken over the ground floor of the house. Norman had taken refuge in the basement with the TV on.

"I remember her just, completely, falling apart," said Lynn. Marion was beside herself. Steve had been taken away from her. He abandoned her. The tears, the music, the heartbreak and the anger created such a scene that when a few of Lynn's friends dropped by that night, they immediately fled into the basement to sit with Norman. Lynn stayed with her mother, trying to calm her down, while her father and the friends sat downstairs, waiting out the storm.

Most of Marion's grief, the moments she still remembers, were quiet, private ones. She would cry behind the steering wheel on her morning drive to work. Then she'd fix her makeup and hair in the rear-view mirror before heading into the office with a smile on her face. This ritual was the basis for an expression I grew up hearing: "You don't know the tears shed behind the steering wheel." I thought it was a reference to a song or movie.

Each of the Goodayles had their own version of reconciling the hole Steve left. They dealt with their grief without fanfare or much conversation, so it wasn't surprising when Marion made a unilateral decision without talking to Norman or Lynn about how they'd remember Steve.

***

No one recalls when the picture of Steve appeared on the wall, but they agree on who hung it: Marion.

It happened sometime after renovations at the cottage were finished around 1980, while Lynn was away from her parents for the first time in Edmonton. Marion had been going through Steve's photo album and stopped at the photo of him sitting on the couch during Christmas 1976. She thought it was a "lovely picture" and, if she was going to hang a photo of Steve, "that was the last one that we had."

She had it blown up, framed and the next time she and Norman went up to the cottage, she hung it there – because Steve had loved the cottage. She chose the spot over the doorway for a reason so obvious that she chuckled when I asked: "So we can see it."

The 12-foot doorway is directly opposite the main entrance to the cottage. Though it's high up, if you were looking ahead, perhaps out towards the windows and the water, your gaze might track upwards and catch the eye of the 17-year-old boy looking back at you.

On Lynn's next visit to the cottage, the first thing she saw was her brother. "Oh, you've got the picture of Steve up," she thought, but didn't say out loud. His presence was a declaration, not a point of discussion. The Goodayles had reached a new stage.

- - -

E.K. HUDSON is a writer and researcher based in Dubai. Her work is mostly about people's inventions and the cities they call home. Follow her work at ekhudson.org

POSTSCRIPT

This story began with a question: Who was my Uncle Stephen? I'd heard stories about him over the years, but they were scattered pieces of a bigger narrative I'd never heard in its entirety. My mom and my grandma would share memories of Stephen when something jolted a memory to the forefront of their minds, or when someone directly asked about him.

Here's what I knew when I began working on this story: My uncle had died in a car crash after a day of skiing. He was the only one killed. My family felt that the system hadn't done justice to his death; my family alleges that the drivers of the car that collided with them were drunk. There was an open case of beer in the back, they say, and the two men didn't stay at the scene. Allegedly, they fled to a nearby cafe to drink coffee and, because they were friends with the local cops, avoided any charges. This was initially the story I set out to tell: Was my family wronged by the system? I wanted to find out the truth.

The first call I made was to the Collingwood police, the force who responded to and investigated the accident. That call was enough to realize that verifying the story of the drunk drivers was going to be nearly impossible – the police department destroys files after 20 years. My uncle died on January 20, 1978. Doing this story almost 40 years later, not only were documents gone, but the people involved are gone too. The driver of the car my uncle was in, Andrew Scheve, died a few years ago and I never found the drivers of the other car. The lack of documents and people made me reflect; I realized that a potentially unjust court case wasn't the story I was trying to tell anyway. The core of why I chose this photo is because I'd wanted to know who my uncle was and better understand my mom and grandma. Once I settled on this direction, my guiding questions became obvious: Who was he, and why is that particular picture of him hanging in a lofty doorway in our cottage?

I relied on documents my grandma had saved, family photos and, of course, memories – both my own and that of my family's. The hardest part was realizing how memories either disappeared or changed over the course of the 40 years since Steve died. My grandma's memory in particular has changed in comparison to my mom's and Peter's. At first, I was worried, especially after speaking with her in a rare moment of candid reflection one night. It was suddenly clear that she really believed Steve's death was "beautiful," which felt disturbing after learning from Peter how it really happened. But how do I tell one of my favorite people that I can't fully trust her memory? In the end, my mom helped me, of course. She told me over the phone, after my tear-filled explanation of my dilemma, to just write the facts - memories change but facts cannot be disputed. Granny knew Steve didn't die instantly, they all did, but her memory has changed. That said, though, the strength of her conviction today left me with a question: How can we ever trust our memories?

4 Word Blind

I did second grade twice, and wasn't sure if I was moving on to third.

By Francesca Carter

I'm eight years old and am smiling in this photograph, even though I am not happy. I am in second grade for the second time because I cannot read. School is like hell. Every day I am there I become so anxious I get hot flashes and my chest tightens. I never think of raising my hand. I daydream and want only to go home.

By summer I still cannot read. Most kids learn to read in kindergarten and especially by second grade. I can memorize any story you read to me, but I cannot read a single word of *Good Night Moon*, let alone *Harry Potter*, which is all I wanted to read.

By the summer my parents are desperate. My teachers cannot understand how I learn. I have been through seven different programs, none of which have succeeded in teaching me to read. Now I am in yet another.

I am driving home with my dad when we pass a road sign. The sign has two words, each with two letters. The sign is a mystery to me.

At the end of the previous summer, my parents told me that I wouldn't be moving on to third grade with the rest of my classmates and friends. Already shy, I rapidly sank into a state of constant fear, worried I would say the wrong thing, get the wrong answer and look stupid. I barely acknowledged my friends. I remember feeling so ashamed that I told myself I would never do anything ever again that would make me feel embarrassed. So I became ever more quiet, shy and withdrawn.

The first day of my second time in second grade, my mom walked me to school. Before we left home, she cried. I didn't cry –I said absolutely nothing. I only knew I was being held back because I had something called "dyslexia." My parents had explained to me it was just another way of learning. But in my mind I knew it was a diagnosis of stupidity.

Being held back a grade wasn't the first time I'd stood out as "abnormal" to my classmates and myself. I'd already shuffled through two years of being pulled out of class at random times by random adults forcing me take random tests and asking me a billion random questions - a few of which I actually liked - but most of which just made me feel even more stupid and frustrated.

"What is an island?" one lady asked me.

"An island is an island." I said.

She asked me to elaborate.

"I don't know." I said.

The questions and tests were intended to determine how I learned. They created what is called an IEP - an "Individualized Education Program"—a plan that was suppose to "catch me up" to my peers, to help me "learn." The IEP allowed me to take tests outside the classroom, to have longer time on assignments, and also meant me being pulled out of class several times a week for special ed. Teachers would try to teach me how to read. But in my head, they just labeled me as someone different, someone "stupid."

Recently my mother came across over 100 pages of my IEP. They contained mostly scores from tests with strange names and transcriptions of observations, analyses, conclusions, and recommendations from teachers, psychologists, speech therapists, audiologists and vision therapists all based on how I responded to their tests and questions. I feel they would be surprised, if not shocked, if they found out how and what I'm doing today. These people never saw me overcome my reading problems, test out of my IEP or go on to college and graduate school. And for some reason, I imagine that they thought I would never amount to much – or maybe that's because, at that point in my life, *I* didn't believe I would become anything.

Dyslexia is the ultimate shape shifter. It manifests itself in a number of different ways with varying and inconsistent symptoms. After talking with neuroscientists, I realized that they themselves don't agree on a definition. What they can agree on, however, is that dyslexia can make it painfully difficult for some people to learn to read.

William Graves, a neuroscientist at Rutgers University, who studies the brain and reading, told me that the core problems with dyslexia are not visual or a reflection of a lack of understanding, but rather are actually a problem with associating letters to sound—speech to sound.

At the end of my second year of second grade, I had made little progress in terms of my reading. I had gone through speech therapy, vision therapy and even more tests—my teachers, the psychologists, and my special ed specialists were all struggling to understand how my brain worked. During an IEP meeting with the school, my mom, having lost patience, angrily said, "You still don't know how my daughter learns."

Up until this point in my life, school was a constant struggle. And it didn't stop when the bell rang at the end of the day. When I came home my mom would make me a snack and an hour later I would pull out my homework. My dad would sit with me and together we would tackle what should have been a 30-minute worksheet, but which would inevitably turn into four to five hours of torture. My dad tried every which way to get me to understand and finish my homework. I would try for the first hour or so and then eventually I would start to cry. I would throw myself off my chair, and scream, "I'm stupid. I can't do this!"

My dad would patiently calm me down, tell me that I was smart, and that we just hadn't figured out how I learned. And then for the 30th time that evening he would re-explain my homework in a new way, hoping I would finally understand the math word problem and the science questions.

This happened every day, and every day he didn't give up on me. He would tell me over and over again, "Francesca, one night you'll be in bed reading your favorite book under your covers with a flashlight long after bedtime, and I'll have to come in and yell at you to turn off the flashlight and go to sleep." I would always shake my head, never believing him.

My dad started tutoring kids as a freshman in college, when he volunteered to tutor 4th graders in a Latino neighborhood of San Francisco. Nearly 20 years later, after an injury ended his career as a firefighter/paramedic, he began working at a tutoring center that focused on kids with learning disabilities. And a few years after I was born he got his teaching credential and became a middle school science teacher. He only lasted seven weeks. As my dad always says, "I could handle a five-car pileup with major injuries on the freeway, but I had no clue how to manage 35 middle schoolers at a time. I'm just better at teaching one-on-one."

He eventually did do one-on-one tutoring again; but his only client was me.

But no matter how much my dad worked with me after school, or how much I was pulled out of my classroom, I wasn't learning how to read. And when my mom confronted my IEP specialists, they finally acknowledged they had no clue how I learned.

So my parents decided to do something extreme: send me to a tutoring center for three months at a cost of $11,000. It was called Lindamood-Bell Learning Processes.

Lindamood-Bell isn't exactly a tutoring center. It's a place where kids like me go to learn to read. The program was created by a reading specialist and a speech pathologist. They do an intense three -and four -hour tests of each child to determine a specialized program they will put the child through for the summer (or for some, during the school year).

I remember going five days a week for four hours a day. I hated it. I begged my parents not to make me go. I was tired at that point, and had given up on ever being able to read. A week before I started at Lindamood-Bell my dad bribed me: he told me that every day I attended I would get a roll of quarters. I didn't comprehend at the time the amount of money that actually was. All I knew is that it allowed me to "buy" those plastic rings from those gum-ball machines at the supermarket. Of course after I had "bought" fifty rings I got bored and started saving my money to buy *Harry Potter* paraphernalia.

On top of the roll of quarters, during my 15-minute breaks my mom or dad would bring me an Einstein chocolate chip bagel with cream cheese, the highlight of my day.

I don't remember a lot from Lindamood-Bell, but what I do remember is someone holding a mirror in front of my mouth and telling me to go through the vowel sounds - over and over again. They told me that until I could differentiate the vowel sounds, I wouldn't be able to sound out words while I was trying to read.

Recently, I wanted to know more about the Lindamood-Bell processes and what my memory with the mirror was about. I spoke with Cara Nemchek, the director of their New York City center. She told me that what I did with the mirror was part of their *LiPs* Program. She explained that it was about "articulatory feedback: what does it feel like in your mouth to make certain sounds?"

She also reminded me of another program I went through called *Seeing Stars*. I would write words in the air with my finger - either given to me verbally or with a flashcard. Some of them were real words, some of them were "nonsense words." But they helped me learn to picture words in my mind's eye.

Still, by midway through that summer, I had made very little progress. My parents worried that they had spent all that money on yet another dead end. I was also miserable; I wanted to be playing with my friends, not stuck inside trying to learn. I didn't know until years later that my parents had decided that if I didn't show any improvement in another week they were going to pull me from the program.

And so it was that one-day my dad was driving me home one day from Lindamood-Bell. I was in the back seat of our van, staring up at the road signs as they passed, doing what I usually did: hoping a miracle would happen and I could read one of them.

We neared the exit to our house, and I saw the sign
"Del Mar Heights"
I started to say what I had read.
"Delllll. Maaarrrr...mm-a-rrrr...."
Then, "Heigghhhtttsss..."
Even now, 17 years later, I do not recall exactly what I shouted to my father in my excitement. What I do remember is that, a month later, I was no longer staring at road signs, menus, books, and worksheets and praying/dreaming/hoping I would somehow be able to read them; I was reading *Harry Potter*.

- - -

Francesca Carter *is a long-form narrative writer and documentary filmmaker. You can see her work at: francescacorinnecarter.com*

POSTSCRIPT

When my professor told me to pick a photo that I would eventually write a story about, I didn't know which photo to use. But I did know which childhood event the photo would portray.

I've always cherished my aunt and uncle's 50th wedding anniversary as one of the best memories from my childhood. But it wasn't until recently that I realized that event/memory occurred during one of the worst times in my life. I was eight years old, had just been forced to repeat second grade, was depressed and beginning to have suicidal thoughts. Getting to dress up in a green, velvet dress with puffy sleeves, made me feel like a princess and provided the escape from reality I desperately needed.

That memory and photo carried me to eight months after the photo was taken - to the summer I learned to read. In order to remember and reconstruct that summer and the events that led to it, I wrote down my own memories, interviewed my parents, talked to neuroscientists about how the brain learns to read, and lastly, talked to an expert from Lindamood-Bell Learning Processes - the program that helped me learn to read. Most importantly, I had my mother send me over 100 pages of my IEP - my Independent Educational Plan - along with the notes that different professionals used to describe and evaluate the way I learned.

5 DISOBEDIENT

I was my father's daughter. Then I brought home my child.

By Francine Parham

I was the good daughter. I obeyed when my parents spoke; especially my father. I grew up in a family where doing what you were told was not just expected, but required. There were consequences if you disobeyed.

In December of 1987 I returned home for winter break from college. I was a junior at Purdue and hadn't been home in over a year. It was expensive getting from West Lafayette, Indiana to upstate New York and, in truth, I liked being away. I did not have to follow the rules at school. I was having fun, too much fun.

I flew home and my mother picked me up at the airport. We chatted in the car about nothing in particular, and when we arrived home my brother, Oscar, helped me carry my bags in.
Everyone was home – my three sisters and two brothers. I was not thinking about them. I was thinking about my father.

My mother opened the front door and my father, who had been in the kitchen, came out and for moment he looked confused.

I did not look at him as I walked through the door but I could hear his voice.

"What the hell is that?" he asked.

"His name is Christopher and he is my baby," I heard myself say to my father. "He is mine - my child." My father just looked at me.

No one spoke.

O scar Parham, Sr. was a provider. That's how he demonstrated his love for his children. He often worked two jobs to take care of us, and sometimes a third one if he could squeeze it in on the weekends. He only knew hard work. We wanted for nothing materially.

He was the son of a sharecropper and his mother picked cotton in the fields of Virginia. He was the youngest of seven children. He was the only child of his parents' who went to college.

My parents were teachers, a noble profession with little pay. We were expected to perform in school. They expected nothing less from us, especially my father.

Only years later did I realize how much I was my father's child. I was the oldest of his six children. He even named me in the hospital when I was born - after a model in a French magazine. My mother said she was okay with it.

There were times in my childhood when my father and I were inseparable. In high school, he dropped me off every day as he headed to his school. He also picked me up after school in his Corvette. We talked a lot during those drives. Sometimes he drilled me about how I was doing in school. Sometimes I just looked out the window listening to his rhythm and blues music.

He would hold me up to my siblings as a model of hard work: I went to school, came home and studied. I caused no problems and had friends that he and my mother approved of. I worked hard to get good grades. My father often told me I was smart, but I felt that wasn't the case. I would hear him sometimes tell my sister, "If you had Francine's gumption combined with your smarts, they couldn't stop you." She was the smart one. I had to work hard to gain his approval. My father was happy as long as you got the results he thought you should.

W e stared each other down for what seemed like forever. I had not taken my coat off because I was afraid he would tell me to leave. I had been told to leave before, so I expected this. I left home, came back and learned to keep my mouth shut.

I wanted to run, but I couldn't. So I stood there as he began to speak.

Christopher was a year and a half old. I had hidden my pregnancy from my family. I planned to complete college and only then tell my family that I had a child. But my plans fell apart when my mother happened to call me at work when I wasn't there.

Tanya, my supervisor, told my mother that I had taken Christopher to the pediatrician for a checkup. When I returned, Tanya told me that my mother had called and what she had said. I said nothing. My mother didn't call me for three days. I didn't call her either. We talked almost every day even if only for five minutes. I spent those three days trying to figure out how I was going to cover up what Tanya told her. I had never lied to my mother. Finally, on the fourth day, my phone rang. I knew it was her.

"Francine, I heard you had a baby," she said.

I told her I had and then I started to cry.

"This is not the time to cry, Francine," she said. "You now have someone to take care of. It's not just you anymore."

Then she said, "I'm on my way."

She arrived a week later and embraced Christopher. She had only told my father that she was going to visit me, just to check in. She asked no questions.

She did tell one person about Christopher—my brother Oscar. And even then she kept the secret for months. "Momma only told me about Christopher on the day you brought him home," my brother would recall.

Now, as my brother passed my father heading to the living room, my father grabbed his shoulder as he walked by. My father almost lost his balance when he saw my brother holding a baby. My father would later say that he thought it was my brother's child. I didn't know until years later that my sisters had gathered at the top of the stairs peering down as my father began to speak.

"Well your life is fucked up now," I heard my father say. "How could you be so stupid?"

I said nothing. We had all been called stupid at one time or another. We were used to that.

"What are you going to do now?" he asked.

I said nothing.

"How are you going to take care of a baby?"

Again, I said nothing.

My sister Nikki, who was then 17, would later tell me how confused she was. "We saw you as you walked in from the top of the stairs, but Oscar was holding a baby," she said. "We didn't know who the baby belonged to and thought it was Oscar's baby. We thought that maybe you were keeping a baby for him."

"I was 15 at the time and remembered saying to Nikki, I think Francine has a baby," said my sister Lisa. "Wow."

Little did they realize that as they made their way down the stairs they also would be subjected to my father's anger.

I finally sat down. My two sisters and brother were now on the couch side-by-side beginning to listen to my father's diatribe.

My son was stumbling around the house playing and laughing with my youngest brother. My mother was in the kitchen.

"When you get up in the morning, you can go back to school but you're leaving the baby," my father bellowed.

That was it. He was done. He had made a decision that, as always, I was to follow without question. Then he went to bed.

That night as lay in my bed I could not sleep. I had decided that I needed to do something. But the problem was, I had spent all my life doing not what I wanted to do, but doing what he told me to do. I was living his dreams, his hopes and desires. I was doing exactly what he wanted me to do, and being who he wanted me to be.

I didn't even like college, but it was my escape – just as it was his from his family, a long time ago.

The following morning I packed my one large suitcase, preparing to leave. I was leaving, as my father instructed me to do, but not without my child. I was determined not to allow this. I was lugging my suitcase down the stairs with my coat wrapped around me when I heard a voice behind me. "Where are you going?"

"I'm going back to my home," I told my father. "I'm going back to Indiana."

"You can go," he said, "but the baby stays here."

As a child I would have not said a word and more than likely complied. But this time it was different. Before I could think, I said defiantly, "No I'm not leaving my baby. If I go, Christopher goes too and if I stay he stays too."

I waited for something to happen, but nothing did. My father had no response. He simply lifted my suitcase and took it back to my room. I followed because Christopher was in the room. I didn't know what to expect. He set my suitcase down without looking at me and went back to into his bedroom. I closed my door and he did the same. I heard nothing. The house was quiet and so was my son. He lay sleeping through it all.

Later that morning and for remainder of the week I was at home. It was as if nothing had ever happened. We celebrated Christmas. We ate a lot. My father played with my son, sang to him and made him laugh. We all laughed, even though only two days earlier my house had been filled with tension and anger.
But something had changed: I was willing to accept the consequences for not following his rules, his expectations. For the first time in my life, I had spoken up to the father I had always feared but whose approval I always wanted.

I felt I had become an adult in my father's eyes. In an unexpected way, I think my father tried to guide us in the right direction. He just didn't always know how. He believed that if he made all the rules, we would succeed. He always said that he had seen much more than we had. He knew better.

He would often say, "I'm not telling you what someone told me, I'm telling you what I know."

In the end, I took Christopher back to school with me. He went to daycare while I worked and went to class. Two years later I graduated, went to graduate school, and then, when I began to work, my parents, who had grown close to Christopher, volunteered to have him live with them so that I could begin my career. I came home every month, if not more often, until he graduated from high school, all the while living with them.

My father never scolded me again. Sometimes he would jokingly ask, "Any surprises for us?"

"Nope daddy," I'd reply.

- - -

FRANCINE PARHAM *is a business professional. She speaks and writes about career success and the important lessons she learned along the way. Read more on francineparham.com*

POSTSCRIPT

There are people and events that shape your life and forever change who you are. They test you. My first test was my father.

The picture of my father in his Corvette evoked the memory of our countless conversations we had and one of the most important ones - bringing home my child for the first time. That conversation we had would forever shape for the rest of my life, who I would become and more importantly what I stood for.

I would forever take ownership of my actions and demonstrate courage in the midst of uncertainty and even fear realizing that I may have to pay a price for doing so. I came to realize that the price maybe losing your family; your livelihood; your friends; things you may have worked to achieve all of your life or that you treasure deeply.

Thankfully I did not have to make that decision about my family, but would be tested in many facets of my life going forward.

With all of my father's flaws, I learned perseverance from him and most importantly I found my strength and fortitude to stick to what I believe in, even when I am scared. I may have never known I had in me the ability to stand up if I had not been forced to confront him. We all have defining moments in our lives that shape our character.

My father is no longer alive having died almost two years ago just prior to me starting Columbia. Just as he had watched me come into the world, I watched him leave the world. He lived with me prior to his death.

I think he would be proud to know that I acknowledge him for the courage he taught me to have and that he tested my courage - something that I will always treasure in my life. I've had many tests since then and survived them all.

My disobedience paid off. My father was my biggest test.

I passed.

6 Path of a Bullet

My grandfather's life was a mystery to me. But maybe he was closer to me than I knew.

By Elise Hansen

All I knew of my grandfather growing up was that he died in a hunting accident before I was born. I didn't know his name, and I didn't know what he looked like—I'd never seen a picture of him. It wasn't until last year, on a mountainside in Montana, that I learned that the one thing I did know about him might not be true. We were on a family vacation; I was hiking with my mom along a trail strewn with wildflowers and scratchy with evergreens. I asked her what my dad's parents had been like. My grandfather's death, she finally told me, may not have been an accident.

Her answer took me aback. But it would be over a year until I began asking more. Who was this man, my grandfather? Was this why my dad never talked about him? And what did his death have to do with a cold night four years ago as I stood barefoot on my neighbor's porch?

My dad does not talk about his parents. So I first went to my mom. "Random question," I texted her, "what's dad's dad's name (my grandfather)?"

I expected to recognize his name. I expected to think, "of course! I knew that." But when she replied, "William Jerit Hansen," the chimes of remembrance didn't so much as whisper. It was a starting point, though.

You can learn a lot about a person with just their name, a vague notion of geography and a couple of estimated dates. I found some records and I started calling my dad's family.

William "Bill" Hansen was born in Milwaukee, Wisconsin, in 1932. He grew up in Milwaukee, too, in one of the apartments in a six-story complex owned by his grandmother. He probably lived there his entire childhood, until he was 18 and left for college. As a senior in high school, he was on the football team, the swim team, the student paper, and was the basketball team manager. According to the caption in his high school yearbook, anyway. Someone put a digitized version of the 1949 Riverside High School yearbook online; finding it was like rooting through the dusty, cobwebbed corners of Google's attic. They probably left it there for the same reasons they would keep the attic copy: it's a signpost to another era, although no one will likely visit again.

In this case, though, it worked: it pointed me to the first picture I'd seen of my grandfather. The young man in the yellowed headshot was fairly handsome: tall, lantern-jawed and not terribly distinctive. He looks nothing like my father.

Shortly after he sat for this photo, Bill went to college at University of Wisconsin at Madison, where he joined ROTC and a fraternity, majored in engineering and met his future wife. Marian Jones was smart, social and funny. She was an English major, yet her speech was peppered with colloquialisms: "water off a duck's back," she'd say, or later, when my aunt was having a dramatic teenage moment, "you should be on a stage! and there's one leaving in ten minutes."

Bill and Marian graduated college in the same class, and not long after, an announcement appeared in Marian's hometown paper, the *Chicago Daily Tribune*:

> *"Mr. and Mrs. Maldwyn L. Jones…announce the marriage June 27 of their daughter, Marian Ruth, to William Jerit Hansen…"*

It was 1953, and the Korean War was drawing to a close. Bill joined the army and headed down to a military base in Augusta, Georgia, where he became a member of the military police. His main duties, my aunt told me, probably involved scooping up soldiers who got too drunk.

"He would have been pretty good at it, I think," she said, perhaps with those drunken soldiers in mind. "He was always willing to overlook things."

This quality would come in handy later, while she and my dad were growing up and learning what they could get away with. But it may also have marked the path to his undoing.

A fad captured the nation in the 1960s and '70s: the tennis boom. Pro tournaments were broadcast on some of the few publicly-available TV channels, piping tennis into homes across the nation, and pro players became nationally-known icons. Tennis belonged to the spry and the hobbling, to men and women, to athletes at home and athletes abroad. Across the country, tennis courts were sprouting up, nets unfurling, straight white lines delineating the play. Tennis courts overran not just the country clubs, but every neighborhood rec center too, and groups of eager players were swarming them.

Bill Hansen returned to Milwaukee after his military stint, a few years before the tennis craze ignited. He and Marian moved into a little house in the Whitefish Bay area, next to the local high school. Marian worked as an English teacher for a few years, and Bill joined forces with a charismatic friend from college. Harry Humphries was a tall, charming, bagpipe-playing Scotsman who was working in what could perhaps be described as the residential asphalt business, paving driveways around the county. Bill joined him, and together, the two became Humphries-Hansen Inc. When forehands and backhands started translating into dollars, they shifted into surfacing tennis courts and running tracks.

They struck the golden days of tennis court paving. Bill went to conferences in Mexico to meet with tennis court contractors; he saw tennis courts made of carpet and the tennis school run by legendary coach Nick Bollettieri. Humphries-Hansen did the tennis courts for Bollettieri's summer camp in Wisconsin and the private tennis courts of Green Bay Packers quarterback Bart Starr, a local deity. Bill designed a special warehouse to process the tennis court paint. It was like Willy Wonka's chocolate factory, but the labyrinth of pipes and barrels and mixers poured out court paint instead of molten chocolate.

My dad worked at Humphries-Hansen for a summer. He rolled barrels of tennis court paint around and squeegeed it across the courts.

"I probably inhaled enough carcinogens to last me the rest of my life," he said. Product safety standards weren't much of a thing at the time. Still, it explains his fastidious preference for well-maintained, well-made tennis courts. And growing up with a surface engineer for a father may also have inspired the pride he took in our immaculate Emerald Zoysia lawn. He loved it because it looked neat and orderly and very green.

Like my dad, Bill was a kindly, generous father, with rarely a harsh word for anyone. He and my dad went on fishing trips; they'd rent a little motor boat for a day and go out on Oconomowoc Lake and cast their lines. They fished for bass, crappies, muskies ("fierce tigers of the deep," my dad calls them), walleye and northern pike. The family vacationed in Canada and Florida, and the family farm, owned with extended family, provided hours of entertainment. They drove tractors around and shot guns at things. Bill and Marian decided the property needed more woods, so they planted row upon row of saplings. Every time they went out to the farm, they'd be there, digging holes and nestling young trees into the ground. They planted the trees in rows, like a nursery, but no one ever moved them as they grew larger. To this day, there is a veritable forest of black walnut and oak trees on the property, all in unnaturally linear formation and too close together.

Those are the times my dad prefers to remember, and his memories are hued with deep fondness. But the tennis court gold rush didn't last, and neither did Humphries-Hansen. Demand for new courts and new athletic tracks evaporated seemingly overnight, leaving the company overstretched and underprepared. Harry Humphries didn't live to see its decline: he had long suffered from bouts of depression, and one afternoon in 1979, he took his shotgun and blew his brains out in the bathroom. The lasting impression that trickled down to my aunt and my dad was one of horror, as his family found the mess and coped with the grief.

Bill and Harry had perhaps been a bit casual about the bookkeeping, and over the next few years the money seemed to disappear (some in the family blame a dishonest accountant). One by one, the other employees of Humphries-Hansen started to leave, until only Bill was left. He started coming home from work earlier and his drinking became more evident. Bill and Marian had always been a social couple; they both drank regularly and smoked profusely. But Bill's alcohol use slipped toward abuse. He started to forget things. My dad was in law school by this time, and during one break he came home and they made plans to go out to breakfast. It was a familiar place, one that Bill drove by almost every day, but when they got there, my dad realized it had been boarded up and closed for weeks. Bill either hadn't noticed or hadn't remembered.

It's funny, the things we choose to remember, and the different values we assign to death. We put so much weight on how people die: we think all their strength and struggles bind together in a moment of illumination, and all their most enduring traits come to the fore.

Or we choose not to measure a life by death. At funerals or in those conversations where we're grasping for assurance or trying to steady our feet on the memory of happier times, we say to each other, "Let's not remember her in those final weeks. Let's remember what she was like before..." We choose what we want to remember.

But how do you reconcile a life that ends in uncertainty? How do you decide what to believe about that life, and death?

On June 8, 1984, Bill Hansen returned home from a hunting trip. No one else was home. Marian and Cathy Ann were out of town; my dad was studying for the bar exam in Virginia; their cousin Nancy, who was staying the night, was out to dinner. Bill got out of his truck and walked around back to collect his gun from the trunk. There was a gunshot. An ambulance arrived shortly. He died soon after.

That is the bare set of facts everyone can agree on. But there are different interpretations of the details. Some in the family believed he had committed suicide. After all, his business was ruined, he was depressed and drinking too much, he died by his own gun in his own driveway. Besides, Bill was proficient with guns, and careful. He would never leave a shell in the chamber, never be caught with the safety off.

On the other hand, there was no note, the gun was still partly in its case, the bullet entered his torso. He may have been drinking, which would have made him more likely to be careless. But if this was his plan, it was an exceptionally mediocre one.

The questions that lingered in the wake of his death weren't ones that go away easily.

What if I had been there? one relative asked. Would things have been different?

Wouldn't he have thought about us before doing things this way? asked another.

What was going through his mind? asked still another.

If death can happen so suddenly, who might be the next person I know to vanish?

Concluding that Bill's death was a suicide may fit the facts, but it doesn't fit with how his children understood him. He was too gentle and considerate to choose such a violent and disturbing death. Ultimately, my father, my aunt and their cousin Nancy have chosen to believe it was an accident. There's a reasonable range of facts to support their conclusions, but I think at the end the day we choose to believe what we can bear to know.

"The alternative would be too painful, I guess," my dad said.

When I first learned on that day hiking with my mother that my grandfather may have committed suicide, a part of me froze. I knew there was some mental illness on my mom's side, but I never knew that depression ran in my dad's family, too. It's different, learning that something that flooded you for so long flows from two tributary streams.

One chilly winter night when I was home on a break from college, I was sitting on my neighbor's couch, pet-sitting. I don't remember what set it off, exactly, but suddenly I was shaking all over. I ran outside and stood in our driveway, staring at my parents' house in the dark. The only thing in my mind was an image of those old guns we kept in the basement. I wanted to shoot myself in the driveway with one of those guns—Bill's gun, as it happens. I don't know how long I stood there, barefoot and cold, staring into the dark at our house. Eventually I went back inside.

Probably just as well; in retrospect, that would have been both logistically tricky and pretty rough on my dad. But I didn't know it would have been déjà vu, and that is what frightens me. What kind of ghosts slide through our thoughts that we are unaware of?

How is that possible that we can re-enact family history without even knowing it? It's disconcerting, piecing together the shards of the past only to find a cracked image of yourself staring back.

Authors Note: Fortunately, while the past may reflect us, it does not control us. Tracing the path back was unnerving, but on this side of history the ending was different. I've lived to treasure many sunrises since that night, and have felt new life spring up out of something that felt sparse and cold. Bill passed down his loving generosity as well as his griefs, and I choose to pursue the former. My dad has always embodied his father's patience and good cheer, and if there is such a thing as friendly ghosts, I would like to let those slide through my thoughts in abundance.

To my dad: I know you will hate that I dwelt on the bad, but I think there were some things that needed to be reckoned with. It's better to face the future with eyes open to the past, better to know what's behind in order to know where to begin.

- - -

ELISE HANSEN *is just as likely to be caught coding as writing or interviewing. She branched out for this piece, but usually writes about the intersection of data and social issues. Follow her at medium.com/@ceb2191*

POSTSCRIPT

One of the guiding themes of this class was William Faulkner's quote, "Memory believes before knowing remembers." I have no idea what that means, but it sounds smart. Memory, belief, knowing—they're all tangled up somehow, and Faulkner seems to have unwound one configuration. The main thing I learned when reporting this story was that even when we know the whole story, we choose what to remember, and ultimately, that's what guides our beliefs about the past and about ourselves.

My dad, for example, knows the facts surrounding his father's death, but he insists that his memories of his father are almost exclusively the stuff of fond reminisces and fishing trips. That's his choice. I also encountered a lot of stories where people had different recollections of the same event, or no recollection at all of someone else's memory. That's a perfectly normal aspect of human memory, but it made reporting—especially on something long past—different from what I'd encountered in reporting on current events or events from a year or two ago.

Bill's death took place before the digital era, which made records and physical artifacts trickier to unearth. Fortunately, there are many people who have dedicated a lot of time and effort to shifting analog artifacts into the digital space. Whoever put Bill's high school yearbook online—thanks for that.

My mom, my dad, my aunt and their cousin Nancy have many lovely memories of Bill and Marian and were extremely generous with their time in speaking to me about them. I could have written a short book with all the stories they gave me, and I would have loved to. The story I ended up writing is not by any means the only story there is to write. That's one of the perils of one-off journalism: it's impossible to capture every facet of two generations' worth of experience and memory within the frame of a single article. I wrote about the shadow of Bill's story in mine because that was the story I needed to write at this moment. But Bill's life—and his family's life—is so much more. I have yet to discover how to reconcile the fullness of their experience with the narrowness of 2,000 words. When I do find out, you should definitely read it.

7 Where He Lived, Where He Died.

My great-grandfather was going to be a prominent man. But then China changed.

By Michelle Yuxiao Gao

In 2003, when I was 12 years old, my father took me to the village where my great-grandfather was born, and where, in this ruined house, he returned to die alone.

The only thing I can remember from that trip is the small room in this photo. Only later would I learn his story, and how it was that a young man born into a prominent family could die as he did, far from his wife and his children.

What happened to him? Was his fate a result of who he was, or was he simply a man overwhelmed by the great forces of history?

My great-grandfather was born sometime in the early 20th century – no one knows the precise year – to the great Guo family in Shanxi Province, China. The family owned a large tract of land. When my great-grandfather was still young, he inherited the family's land and lived there in a big house.

My great-grandfather's name was Guo Zengxian. His father, whose name is lost to history, was known as *"Guo Juren,"* or "Guo, the First-degree Scholar." That title was bestowed on those few fortunate enough to have passed the entry-level Chinese Imperial Examination. The rare title brought the Guo family fame and prosperity, and land. The family grew wheat, cotton, corn and also harvested dates – which, years later, has become a favorite in my family.

Guo Juren lived during the Qing Dynasty, the last dynasty of imperial China, and his was said to be the last generation of the first-degree scholars. The title was abolished in 1905 when the Qing Dynasty was about to end and modern China was about to rise. It was the end of more than two thousand years of imperial China.

Imperial China was beset by defeat and corruption. It had fought and lost two Opium Wars to the British, which resulted in opium being legalized; Hong Kong had been ceded to the British, and many port cities were forced to open to foreign powers. People started rebelling against the Qing government. Finally, in 1912, Sun Yat-sen established the Republic of China, and Puyi, the last Qing Dynasty emperor abdicated. This is the world into which my great-grandfather was born.

When he was about to enter Peking University – the most elite in the country – students there were beginning to study Marxism, hoping to find a new path for the country. A group of students from Peking University founded the Socialist Youth League of China. My great-grandfather studied law at the university. I do not know if he was caught up in the political ferment.

In 1921, the Communist Party of China was officially founded by the same group of people who founded the Socialist Youth League of China. Around the same time, my great-grandfather finished his studies and returned to his home – and land – in Shanxi Province. He married my great-grandmother. I was told that their marriage was a fully blessed one. My great-grandmother was from a wealthy family as well, the daughter of either a high-ranking warlord or a landowner from out of the province.

They remained happily married for a few years. They lived in the big house on my great-grandfather's land, and had four daughters and a son. My grandmother was the youngest of them, and my great-grandfather's favorite. He named her Guo Anna – a western name.

But then, in 1937, the Japanese occupied China. The streets of the nearest county, Pingyao, once prosperous and busy with small businesses, became empty as the nation was plunged into war. My great-grandfather's world was crumbling. He did not work because he did not want to serve the Japanese occupiers. His marriage began falling apart. He began smoking opium.

But my great-grandmother, I was told, was practical – in surviving wartime, and what followed.

China's troubles did not end with the defeat of the Japanese. The country was soon plunged into civil war between the nationalist government and the Communists. My great-grandfather was a landowner, and the Communists saw landowners as enemies of the peasants. With the defeat of the nationalists, Mao Zedong embarked on an aggressive land reform movement, whose goal was to confiscate landowners' land and fortunes and give them to the peasants. My great-grandmother had been running the house and the land, perhaps as a result of my great-grandfather's opium addiction. So, when the Party's local official came and knocked on the door, it was her who was taken away for "investigation" instead of my great-grandfather. She was kept in custody for only two years, I am told, because the local peasants spoke well of her generosity toward them. Others were executed.

But the land that had been in the Guo family for generations was gone. My great-grandmother, I have come to believe, had probably seen it coming and prepared. Before her arrest she had hidden the family's jewels. When the Party officials released her, she quickly collected the jewels from neighbors she had hidden them with, sold them, and with the money she took her two youngest children to Beijing. My great-grandmother thought their wealth was too conspicuous in the small village of Shanxi Province, and thus the family was naturally vulnerable to persecution; they would be better off in a big city like Beijing, where they could hide their identity and be safe. The three elder daughters, meanwhile, were taken care of by the Communist Party after the Party seized the land. They joined the Party's school.

It was unclear when my great-grandmother divorced my great-grandfather, or if they had ever legally signed divorce papers. With the money from the sale of the jewels, my great-grandmother managed to support both my grandmother and her elder brother until they both finished college. Meanwhile, my great-grandfather became a teacher in Shanxi Province, and level of political sensitivity in China started to escalate. His eldest daughter was said to have risen to a prominent position in the Party. She married another rising Party official when they were still students. When they moved to Chengdu in Sichuan Province a few years later, my great-grandfather left Shanxi Province and lived with them for a while. But because he had been a landowner, my great-grandfather's presence threatened to undermine their position in the Party. They ordered my great-grandfather to stay away from them. My great-grandfather had nowhere to go, and so returned to the small village in Shanxi Province.

He came to Beijing once, in 1963, to visit my grandmother when she was in medical school. They had not seen each other in a long time, but did not even have time for lunch. My great-grandfather simply asked my grandmother if her school life was going well, and talked for a little while in her dorm room. He left Beijing the same day, and returned, once again, to his village.

My grandmother graduated and started working as a doctor, and soon began sending her father five Chinese yuan every month. He had by now become homeless. He ate food given to him by his neighbors. The whole village still recognized him, and they took turns feeding him and giving him a place to stay. Five Chinese yuan allowed him to eat well in a small Chinese village in the 1970s, but my great-grandfather, I learned, would spend all the money at once on alcohol. My grandmother would have to send the money to the head of a local primary school who would give my great-grandfather the money little by little, to prevent him from wasting it all.

On the last day of my great-grandfather's life, he seemed to know that his time had come. He had some uncooked flour dough left with him, that he probably bought from a market in the village earlier in the day. He went to the family that had been helping him in his later years, and left the flour dough wrapped on the steps of their house. He walked back to the small room, that once was in his big house, and died there alone.

I tried my best to gather the pieces of his story, but there are mysteries that I cannot yet answer. My grandmother does not know why, for instance, her father came to visit her that day in 1963. I have no way of knowing what my great-grandfather was thinking, as he wandered the land he owned when he was young. Did he recall once thinking his future would be promising as a law student from the best university in the country? Was he blaming the time he was born, or was he blaming everything else that seemed to undermine his life? Was he wondering how his wife could adjust and thrive in the worst historical time for the family? Or was he simply feeling nostalgic for the old days?

- - -

Michelle Yuxiao Gao *is a feature writer and multimedia journalist. She believes that everyone has a life story worth telling. Learn more about her work at MichelleGao.me*

POSTSCRIPT
I finished editing this story around April 26, 2017. On the same day, stories of I. M. Pei circled on my social media, and I learned it was his 100th

birthday. I. M. Pei was a talented Chinese American architect whom I highly respect. He is best known for designing the glass pyramid, part of the renovation of The Louvre. I looked up his detailed bio, and was once again pulled into contemplation of my great-grandfather's life. It's very arrogant to compare side-by-side my great-grandfather and I. M. Pei, but how can one person die early in misery and the other achieve so much in life, when both of them were born in the same country around the same year? What went wrong? What makes their fates so different?

I tried my best to answer the questions. But I could have answered with more confidence, if my great-grandfather hadn't passed away so early, in his sixties. My great-grandfather spent his last years alone, away from his wife and children, in Liangzhao Village, Shanxi Province. The neighbors and the families who moved into my great-grandfather's big house probably have more clues about his last years than people I can reach out to, but I was tied up in New York and couldn't go back to Shanxi to report on the story. Luckily, my grandmother, my father, and some other distant family relatives have pieces of memory about my great-grandfather. But at some point, they too seemed not to know much about this man, as they conflicted with each other in their recall. My grandmother was the only one I talked to who had lived with my great-grandfather; his other children have either passed away, or are too old to communicate over the phone. After intensive background research on the history, I had to make decisions to write what I believed to be true.

China never stops changing. Not long after my great-grandfather's land was confiscated during land reform, Mao decided that the actual ownership of China's land should be the People, thus the country, but not individuals. Peasants only have the right to use land. They do not own the land. Only after Mao died in 1976, did the Cultural Revolution end, and the country de-escalated the political sensitivity that had built up in the past two decades. A couple of years later, scholars started to study and critique Mao's movements, including the land reform and Cultural Revolution. I do not know if my great-grandfather lived to see the change. It does not add to the story much, but it's symbolic to me if he made it through the worst time in Chinese modern history. I wish he did; otherwise, he was the "shameful" landowner, an identity that he had no choice about and was born into, till his death.

8 The Year of Living Almost Dangerously

I went to Congo seeking adventure. I found something even more frightening.

By Elettra Pauletto

On one of my first mornings in Goma, a city in the Democratic Republic of Congo, I took a picture of a woman walking along the side of the road. She's not dressed like most of the people around her, whose fancy shoes and leather briefcases suggest they're walking to work. This woman is not wealthy, not of the city, and may even have come from one of the nearby camps for the internally displaced, where people from the countryside take refuge whenever fighting erupts in their villages.

She's looking straight at me as I snap the picture, giving me a slight scowl. I think she's angry with me, but I can't be sure. Still, I can't help but think she knows something about me, something ugly. My colleague, Leonello, is also in the picture. He's driving the car we're in and he's looking into the camera too. It looks like he's somewhere between afraid and annoyed. Both faces seem to be reproaching me for my very presence in that car, that city, that country. I would come to see that same expression on face after face throughout the year I spent in Congo, always believing that it represented an accusation.

***

When I was twenty-three years old, I lived for a year in a small house on the edge of Goma, in eastern Congo, less than a mile from the border with Rwanda. The city stands at about 60 miles south of the equator, in a mountainous region where active volcanos threaten to erupt, a methane gas filled lake causes high cases of drownings, and a low level conflict among rebel groups and the army pushes waves of people from the countryside to the city each year. I went there to work for a local non-governmental organization, where I distributed food in camps for displaced persons. But when I first arrived in the fall of 2007, all I could do was wonder what the hell I was doing there and what was making me stay.

The one thing I knew, was that I wasn't there because I wanted to help anyone. I was fresh out of college, I had no practical skills, and even fewer illusions that I could make a dent in a decades-long humanitarian effort that had done little to elevate people affected by conflict. I was there because I wanted adventure. And as sure as I knew I couldn't help anyone, I also believed that my presence couldn't hurt, either. But that's not how I felt by the end of it.

***

I grew up moving back and forth between northern Italy and suburban Massachusetts. In college, I spent short periods studying abroad in England, France and Senegal. I tried acid, cocaine and other drugs, and once got drunk on homemade palm wine. I traveled a lot, and went skydiving and bungee jumping in New Zealand, sailing in Australia, and hiking in the Alaskan wilderness. By the time I graduated UMass-Amherst, I was out of conventional possibilities for excitement. I'd just ended a significant relationship that I'd thought was going to be my everlasting, and I was back in suburban Massachusetts thinking my only option was to get a job in a small town. I needed something to jolt me out of that.

I'd taken some classes in international relations as part of my college degree, and knew about volunteer opportunities overseas. I applied to the Peace Corps. They decided to send me to Senegal, but Senegal is safe aside from a sporadic conflict in its southern region. I found a volunteer program in Rwanda, but the country has been at peace since the Rwandan Patriotic Front took power and reestablished order after the 1994 genocide. Then I found the year-long program in Goma. This city, sprawling westward from the border with Rwanda, was exposed to many different kinds of dangers, and the Italian government was prepared to send me there for free, with a monthly salary, despite my lack of experience. It was dangerous, it was accessible, it was perfect.

***

More than 40 different militias fight, pillage and rape in the North Kivu region, of which Goma is the capital. Much of this can be attributed to the 1994 Rwandan genocide, which in some ways never really ended. It crossed into Congo, where intense hostilities between Hutu and Tutsi ethnic groups—which led to extremist Hutus killing 800,000 Tutsis and moderate Hutus in 1994—combined with animosities between hundreds of other ethnic groups. The conflict can also be linked to the exploitation of mineral resources, which causes different armed groups to fight each other for control of the mines.

That isn't all. An active volcano, Nyiragongo, sits directly north of the city. It last erupted in 2002, when lava crawled down the mountain slope from a side crater and carpeted the city streets, burying the ground floors of many buildings and blowing up gas stations. Geologists say the volcano is due for another eruption, but it's unclear whether this would be another slow encroachment, or whether it would burst forth from the central crater, an open cauldron that releases a constant stream of smoke and gases, and emits an orange glow at night.

Goma sits on the northern edge of Lake Kivu, an exploding lake. At 120 cubic miles of water volume, it contains 16 cubic miles of methane gas, and over 60 cubic miles of carbon dioxide. I swam in this lake many times, and noticed nothing unusual. The gases, in most places, are trapped well below the surface. But if they were to be disturbed by underground volcanic activity, they could be released all at once, suffocating the more than 1 million people who live along the lake's shores.

There are also earthquakes. One night I was woken up by a deep rumbling, a noise that came from my dream at first, and continued well into wakefulness. I listened to the ground move. But it was just one of the many aftershocks that came after a large earthquake the week before, which had killed at least 39 people in Bukavu, a city on the other side of the lake.

A plane once crashed near my house after overshooting the runway, killing 21 people, all of whom had been on the ground milling about a busy market place. The airline that operated it, Hewa Bora, crashed so often that it was known by the people of Goma as the "flying coffin." It was the cheapest civilian airline that flew to the capital Kinshasa, 1,500 miles away and across dense rainforests, and most people using it did not have the luxury to choose life over money. The airline finally folded in 2011, after a crash landing in Kisangani killed 74 people.

**

The safest way to get to Goma, is to fly to Kigali, the capital of Rwanda, and drive three hours through the hills. This avoids two significant perils of traveling in Congo, which are its airlines, and ambushes by rebels or bandits, which occur frequently on the country roads outside Goma.

In contrast, Rwanda is idyllic. On the surface, there is no indication that mass killings took place over 20 years ago. Even in 2007, only 13 years after the genocide, there were no telling signs— the roads throughout the capital were paved and well-maintained, there were business centers and multinational banks and new housing developments, and the grocery stores sold what one might expect to find in any Western European grocery store. The government had recently banned the use of plastic bags to avoid pollution, and the directive was strictly enforced. Upon arriving in the country, airport officials checked my bags, and I wasn't even allowed to keep my shoes in plastic bags to protect my clothing.

Leonello and I spent a few days in Kigali and then headed to Goma. The night before we crossed the border, we stayed in the

Rwandan town of Gisenyi so that we could meet with other Italian aid workers stationed there.

Gisenyi is a sleepy town. Luxury hotels dot a lake front of green, manicured lawns and a long sandy beach. Toward Goma, the beach gives way to a rocky shore, where waves lap quietly under the porches of high-end restaurants and private villas.

The night we arrived, we met Filippo for dinner. He'd been in mine and Leonello's position the year before, and he was going to talk to us about what to expect from Goma. Filippo was garrulous, energetic, and seemed happy to be passing on some of the more exciting details of his life. He wore a thick black earing in one ear, and his beard was slightly unkempt. He was speaking Italian, and his Roman accent, with the doubling of all the consonants, seemed exaggerated to me, as if he didn't want us to miss any part of his fascinating story.

He told us of the time he was ambushed by two rebel soldiers on the road back to Goma. They belonged to the National Congress for the Defense of the People (CNDP), a predominantly Tutsi group led by Laurent Nkunda and backed by Rwanda. Filippo had been traveling with colleagues from the organization Leonello and I would be working with. The group had just visited a child soldier transition center, where former child soldiers live during a three month rehabilitation period before returning to their families. The team had $800 in cash and one cell phone per person.

As the group drove around a bend in the road, they saw two men standing in the middle of it, pointing their guns at the car. The driver wanted to make a run for it, but Juvenal, the team leader, was a cautious person.

Juvenal ordered the driver to stop the car, and the gunmen pulled its occupants out and onto the ground. The rebel soldiers demanded that Filippo and the others hand over all valuables, which they did promptly. But the gunmen were nervous. Their eyes were red, and they looked high, or possibly drunk. They ordered Filippo and the others to lay down in a ditch on the side of the road. They beat one of the other aid workers, a slight woman who worked as a psychologist. They made Juvenal kneel on the road with his hands up, and they pointed an AK-47 at the back of his head.

Then, for whatever reason, the rebels stopped there. They took their loot and left. The team drove back to Goma to report the attack. The aid organization was not pleased, its leadership made some calls, and before too long, Filippo was riding back into the bush with Abbé Claude, one of the organization's affiliates. They arrived at an unremarkable patch of woods. A high-ranking CNDP officer met them and escorted them deeper into the bush. They arrived at a compound surrounded by armed soldiers. Filippo and Claude were taken into a sitting room, given glasses of milk produced by Masisi cows, which famously belong primarily to members of the Congolese Tutsi community. Then walked in Laurent Nkunda, the leader of the most powerful rebel group in eastern Congo at the time, a man who was wanted by the International Criminal Court for crimes against humanity and who at that moment said, "I'm sorry. You can have your things back."

It turns out, Abbé Claude was somebody's cousin. The head of the aid organization in Goma was also somebody's cousin, and in short, these were the close family connections of the organization I was about to start working for. This was no ordinary NGO. It had a role to play in the ethnic animosities that dominated the region, that pitted Rwanda against Congo, and Congolese Tutsis against other ethnic groups.

***

Two days later, Leonello and I were in Goma. On our first night, while our permanent home was being made ready, we stayed in the *prefecture*, a building that acted as part guest house, part dining establishment, and part home to the head of our organization. The doors to each room gave out onto a walkway that overlooked the city, while interior windows looked out onto a quiet courtyard.

We arrived during the day, and by the time I settled in and stepped out again to join Leonello at the walkway, it was night. The first thing I noticed were the street lights ahead. I remembered all the warnings I'd heard from other expatriates who'd lived in Goma before. They all came down to the assessment that "Man, this place is tough." I imagined crime being committed under those streetlamps, thinking I might glimpse an attack, a murder. I was terrified, and I wanted to go home. I didn't want to be there anymore. Why had I come? I scanned the darkness along the side street that led to the prefecture. I examined the tall iron gate that closed off the property to the road, and watched the guards sitting near it. The prefecture, like many residential buildings around Goma, was encircled by a cement brick wall topped with barbed wire. I thought that "tough" meant dangerous things happened all the time. I just wanted to keep my head down, do as I was told, and maybe I'd survive the year.

I caught site of the volcano to my right. In the night, it was nothing but a red halo aloft in pure darkness. To my left Leonello was looking out onto the city. I joined him and we discussed the plan for the next day, the meetings we had to go to, the people we'd meet. We'd go into the office and see where we were going to be working. Someone would show us around town.

"Look at it," I said, with my face turned toward the volcano. "It's like it's fueling all this. All this conflict and hate. Literally fueling it."

"Well, I don't know," said Leonello. "I think that if they all just stopped and contemplated it for a moment, they'd realize they have nothing to fight about."

I knew he was right, but I just couldn't see it that way. I couldn't take my eyes off that floating red glow, that open cauldron casting red strands of light onto the sky, as if monsters were reaching ghostly fingers in sinister supplication to an unfathomable universe. It looked like hell itself. It was surrounded by death. This place was a nightmare. I was terrified.

***

I needed to feel that I was there for a reason other than adventure. I needed to have something to show for my presence. One thing I could do with my limited skill set was sit at a desk and check off names. So I volunteered to help distribute food in camps for people who had been displaced by fighting.

The camps sprawled over fields, volcanic rocks and ancient craters just outside of Goma. Flying above them, you could see clusters of white dots gathered over fields, and next to them, hundreds and hundreds of craters, filled in with vegetation or sometimes water, and varying in diameter and depth. The UN Refugee Agency gave out white tarps to people arriving in the camps, who used them to waterproof their huts of grass and banana leaves.

In some camps, more than 25,000 people lived in these
constructions, so close together they appeared to be on top of each
other.

My the camp I went to most often was called Mugunga II. At the
time, it held about 25,000 people and was the largest. I worked with a
team of Congolese aid workers. We would arrive early in the morning,
around 8 a.m. to set up a table for checking names, while making sure
the trucks piled high with food had arrived and were being unpacked.

My table was their first stop before people could receive their
provisions, which consisted of salt, dried peas, palm oil, and maize.
Those who came to claim were usually women, or children who'd lost
their parents. One day at one of the larger camps, a woman, baby on
back, came up to me in line, bared her breast and shouted at me in
Swahili, pointing repeatedly at me, her breast, and then her baby. I
couldn't understand her words, but it seemed clear she was hungry,
and could no longer produce enough milk to feed her child. She looked
at me, pleading. I could do nothing but stare at her, stare at her breasts,
at her baby. "Watch out for your jacket," said the UN representative I
was working with, referring to the jacket draped over the back of my
chair. "These people will snatch anything as soon as you look away." I
quickly tied the jacket around my waist, but when I turned back the
woman and baby were gone.

My role was simply that of asking for names and checking
them off my list of people who were entitled to food rations. My
team and I sat under the sun most of the day, having eaten nothing
but breakfast at dawn. Still, by the time distribution ended around 5
p.m. I was usually reluctant to eat anything. There was no place to
hide, and children especially stared at me, perhaps curious about my
appearance—white, not Congolese. Once, as the distribution died
down, I attempted, fleetingly, to nab a biscuit from my pocket. I
glanced over and saw a child, crouched on the ground scraping up
the dried peas that had fallen out of some of the bags into the
crevices of the volcanic rock ground. He was staring at me, grinning.
He didn't look upset that I was eating. I felt ashamed.

My Congolese colleagues sometimes became so frustrated by
the long, slow lines that they would yell at the displaced people.
"These country people! They're so dirty. They don't even deserve
this," one of them said to me. "Can't they just take care of
themselves?" He complained that he should get paid a lot better. He

wore shiny new shoes, but I said nothing. I knew that I could leave whenever I wanted. He was Congolese. He might never leave.

The weather was capricious and spells of searing heat and cold to the bone could alternate effortlessly any given day. Women and children huddled under rainbow-colored umbrellas in both sun and rain, staring listlessly at the feet of the food distribution table. Those who could not find shelter stood motionless under the weather, their faces falling as their feet sank ever deeper into grey mud. Nobody cried, but the rain poured down their cheeks as they stared.

Riots often broke out. I was with a team in Rutshuru, a town about 30 miles north of Goma, sitting at my table when a rock landed on the World Food Program truck in front of us, cracking the windshield. Then more rocks came, falling onto the grass in front of us, nearing us with each thump. They were coming from the crowd.

A group of displaced women hustled me to my team's Land Rover. Just then, the rock throwing stopped, a scuffle broke out as angry men made for the maize sacks, and the police launched themselves in. A dense crowd closed in on the table where my team and I had been sitting only moments before.

I hadn't even realized there was a danger of getting caught up in a riot. But it turned out to be even worse than that. When I reached the Land Rover I saw that my colleague Mango was sprawled across the back bench with his head in his hands.

"What happened to you?" I asked him.

"Malaria," he replied. "It's better now the bombing stopped."

"What bombing?"

"You didn't hear? Over there…" he said, pointing to the dipping tree line behind the distribution truck. That's where the jungle started, and behind that, villages.

I recalled the hollow, metallic booming sound from earlier that day. I had thought it was sacks of maize being loaded onto trucks. It was the sound my father's pickup truck made when he loaded cement sacks onto its bed.

As I thought of this, I became aware of a man staring at me through the windows of the Land Rover. He stood alone, a few paces away from the vehicle, wearing a jet black cowboy hat. His suit looked like it had been black too, once. Now it was scuffed with grey marks, and it was slightly oversized, as if he had once filled it, but now his shoulders struggled to keep the jacket aloft. He stood splay-legged with his arms crossed in front of him in a pose he seemed comfortable with.

I locked eyes with him, then looked away. He wasn't fazed by this and kept his attention firmly on me as police descended on the scene of the fight, men in tattered shirts made off with a sack of food, and the rest of my team sprinted for the Land Rover. For the first time I felt afraid, not for my safety, or of the riot outside, but of how this man might judge me. It was the face of the woman in the picture I'd taken, and again what I saw was an accusation: I was safe in the Land Rover and he was not; I didn't even know enough about a life lived in danger to be afraid of rocks thrown at me by people who were hungry and afraid; I had carelessly let those women risk injury to themselves to save me; I was leaving as soon as things turned ugly.

***

After the riot, my team was escorted back to Goma by a convoy of UN soldiers because of reports of fighting along the route into the city. I spent the drive staring into the bushes, alert to any hostile movement, but nothing ever happened. And nothing is what continued to happen.

I grew confident with my surroundings. Meanwhile, as I worked in the camps, Leonello had been tucked away in our little house—a three bedroom place in a compound run by the church— writing articles on the political situation in Congo. It all seemed very official to me, and he was so confident in what he was doing that I felt comforted by his sense of purpose. I could tell myself I was there for a reason.

Before Goma, he was someone I'd had little in common with. He was six years older than me, which at my age, seemed like a lot. He was intellectual and analytical, and I still felt young and careless in comparison. When I ask him about it now, he says I did seem young to him. So when he kissed me on the neck one day at dusk, as I stood outside peeling tomatoes for dinner, I was surprised. It was soft but short, and he pulled away and walked back into the kitchen without awaiting a reaction.

For Leonello, Goma held a certain enchantment, the fascination of a border city, a frontier where civility meets lawlessness. He wishes we'd delved into that more fully together, that sensation of being with another person as you pass from one stage of life to another. Because that is what we were doing. I was learning two things I never really had before: compassion and patience. Yet there were times when I felt harshly toward the displaced people in the camps, just as my Congolese colleagues did. There were so many of them and it took so long to get them processed and it felt like they weren't cooperating. They'd forget their IDs or they'd start arguing. There were some days when I wanted to go back to Goma and eat something, take a shower, and get out of the cold or heat.

I was learning things about myself I didn't like. I had always thought of myself as someone who champions justice and equality, and who understands that poverty and displacement are not choices but products of war and economics. But I wasn't this person.

Leonello also felt like he was losing part of himself, the boy he'd been. Whenever he came to the camps with me, he watched the feet of the displaced people standing line. They wore no shoes, or broken shoes, or flip flops, leaving their feet naked to all the elements and the hard volcanic rocks, unprotected from everything and still holding the weight of each body, each bundle of clothes and soap and maize that were the entirety of a displaced person's material life. Leonello saw this on the one hand, and on the other he knew that the Congolese Tutsi CNDP bore an enormous responsibility for creating displacement, and that the organization we worked for was in some way complicit given the obvious family connections. It hurt him so see the suffering. He left Goma halfway through our program, after which I lived there alone for five more months.

I would like to recall this time as one during which I threw myself into the lives of the people I was helping to feed. That I continued waking at dawn each day, driving to the camps, sitting at a table as thousands of people streamed before me. My Congolese colleagues continued to do this, but I did not. I wrote reports by day and by night I went out to dinner and sometimes to clubs, building a protective shell around myself. I made friends with expatriates who had come to Congo for humanitarian reasons and who spent their evenings partying by the lake.

Adventure is a quick and short-lived sensation that inevitably gives way to settling in. I adapted by ignoring the poverty and displacement I'd seen so that I could still believe in the romance of living in a war zone.

***

On the day I left Congo I waited in a car with a nun. The head of my organization had left us there as he stopped by the office to pick up something before driving me to Kigali, from where I would fly home. The nun was just catching a ride. "Thank you for coming," she said to me as we waited. "It must have been hard for you to leave your comfortable home to come see all this." I was watching a group of fat middle aged men waddle around a van looking very pleased with themselves, their bulbous cheeks poised for chuckles as they put on flak jackets and slapped each other on the backs. They looked like I felt when I'd first arrived looking for adventure. Before I'd seen the children standing in the rain, the naked feet, and the faces of those who seemed to demand more of me. They looked like I felt after I'd built my protective shell, but before I'd torn it down.

"Thank you," I said to the nun. "But I really don't feel like I did anything." Just as I was leaving, the rebels were about to capture the city, the violence in the countryside was worsening, and more and more people were crowding into those camps. Now they would all be hungry again.

The volcano never exploded, nor did the lake, and the danger I had come for—the war—was about to hit the city just as I was leaving. I wasn't going to see any of it, but now I was grateful.

A few weeks before I left, a plane had gone down with sixteen aid workers. All of them—friends, and friends of friends—had died, likely upon impact, when their plane lost altitude in rough weather, and crashed into the jungle not far from Lake Kivu. All those dangers surrounding me and the people that I'd met no longer held any appeal. They were simply frightening, and horrific, just as they'd been all along.

Those faces in the picture, the woman bearing her breasts, the man in the camp. Maybe their expressions weren't accusations. When I asked Leonello about the picture, he said he remembers the day I took it. He reminded me that we would take that road to and from home, even though it was longer than the other road, because it was wider and therefore safer.

Leonello also remembers me behind that camera. He says he knew me at extremes, both delicate as I measured my every word and move, and strong to know how to live alone in a place like Goma. He remembers that I hated going to the market. This is true, I thought it was too crowded, and confusing, and I was afraid of the street urchins who buzzed around our car and asked us for money. Their clothes were so dirty and tattered, and some of them were verging on adolescence, which meant they were probably stronger than me. But these children, I hated them. And I wanted to hurt them for getting in my way. I felt this way for many months, as I grappled with this idea that I hated poor and probably homeless children just because they wanted help from me. This didn't make sense, I wasn't supposed to be like that. And yet there I was.

It took time, but eventually I realized that it wasn't the children I was afraid of. I was afraid of my own reaction. I felt myself reacting to the people around me in ways I'd never expected, with behaviors that I hated seeing in myself.

So I stopped. I started talking to the children. I learned that one way to look at it, was that if I didn't pay them, they'd slash my tires while I shopped in the market. But that a better way to see it, was that if I paid them, they would watch my car and protect it from anyone trying to steal it.

Maybe the woman in the picture had seen in me a capacity for ugliness that I did not yet recognize myself. But after at first adapting to Goma by ignoring what I thought were its flaws, I was now learning to change my very outlook. This meant acknowledging what I did not like in others, and in myself.

- - -

ELETTRA PAULETTO *is a researcher, writer and translator focusing on global politics and human rights. Her writing has appeared in Guernica, Harper's Magazine online, and elsewhere. Find her work at medium.com/ @elettra.pauletto*

To explore the unknown and the familiar,
distant and near and to record in detail
with the eyes
of a child,
and beauty
(of the flesh
or otherwise)
horror, irony,
traces
of utopia or hell.

9 "Journey as a Way of Life"

Carrying the story of a stranger.

By Kate Cough

DAN

This is a photograph of Dan Eldon. The photograph was a gift, one that I have carried with me for years. It is one of the first things I hang on my walls and one of the last I take down. I move often and travel light--it's been over a decade since I've spent more than nine months in any one place--but I have kept this as a reminder of the kind of life Dan lived, and the kind of life I have aspired to.

Dan died on the streets of Mogadishu in 1993. He was 22; it was mid July, no doubt it was ungodly hot. U.S. helicopters strafed a building where they thought clan elders were gathered, the home of lieutenant of General Mohamed Farah Aidid. The strike killed dozens of civilians--women and children among them.

Dan was preparing to leave Somalia. He'd spent months covering the carnage, and he was exhausted. International papers were tiring of the story, and things were increasingly violent and chaotic. Journalists were leaving to cover more profitable wars--Bosnia, Burundi, Sierra Leone. But Dan had stayed, and that day he rushed to take photos of the aftermath of the strike. A group of civilians, anguished by the deaths of their friends and family, chased him through the dusty streets. Dan was fast, but the mob was faster: in a fury, they caught Dan and stoned him to death.

The strike that brought about Dan's death was part of increasingly desperate attempts to corral a situation that was rapidly deteriorating into a tangle of warlords and rebels and blue and green helmets. Less than a year later, in March of 1994, all U.S. troops would be gone: after Paul Watson's photos of a naked American soldier being dragged through the streets of Mogadishu were published in the international papers the U.S. lost its appetite for the war.

Dan died that hot July day alongside three of his Reuters colleagues: Hos Maina, Anthony Macharia and Hansi Krauss. Dan's obituary ran in the British papers and on the wires. They called him "a romantic figure of war journalism for whom an early death sometimes seemed inevitable." More than one said, "His heart was in Africa." Some simply noted his death in the confused string of others: *54 dead, 85 dead, 175 wounded, three journalists, four journalists.*

Aidan Hartley, a journalist and friend of Dan's, wrote an account after his death: a circling Black Hawk helicopter followed Dan as he ran through the streets of Mogadishu. Dan shed his bulletproof vest so he could run faster. And after the mob caught up with him, the same helicopter picked his body up from the dirt and flew it home.

The year before Dan died, wrote Hartley, he made Hartley a photo collage, with a note: "*To Aidan, with mixed thanks for giving me my first exposure to the horror.*" Hartley wasn't in Somalia the day his colleagues were killed. He survived the continent's wars, covering the famine in Ethiopia and the bloodletting in Rwanda. He made documentary films, married, had two children. Hartley settled in Kenya and became a cattle rancher, finding "solace in cows and family." And in 2003 he wrote a book: *The Zanzibar Chest*. It was this book that would lead me to Dan.

My copy of *The Zanzibar Chest* is held together with elastic, covered in pen, and a whole section has simply fallen out. The pages are soft from years of reading and re-reading. There are poems and drawings and quotes from friends in the margins that make little sense to me today.

But one story has always stuck in my mind: Dan's first day in Mogadishu, and the group of Reuters stringers he was with, including Hartley, had gone down to the "green line," an imaginary line dividing north and south Mogadishu. "The area between them has become a ghost town, haunted by the memories of splendor and of failure," wrote Diana Schemo in the New York Times.

According to Hartley's recollection of the day:

> Dan got cheeky to a teenager who thought the rocket-propelled grenade launcher in his hands entitled him to the respect of all. The youth lost his temper and pointed at Dan, ready to pull the trigger.... I urged Dan to put his camera down. He ignored me to my alarm and opened his photo bag, from which he fished out a rubber monster mask I had seen in his room at home and slipped this onto his head. It had warts and wrinkly skin and green hair and when Dan stuck his pink tongue out of the little mouth hole the gunman brought his tirade to an abrupt halt with a yelp and a giggle.

In so many accounts of Dan his memory buzzes with life: selling t-shirts he made printed with Black Hawk helicopters on the beaches of Mogadishu; driving an old Land Rover to donate thousands of dollars to a refugee camp in Malawi, breaking hearts with his wide, easy smile. In an interview with the Los Angeles *Times* years after his death, Dan's mother described him like this: "He was a totally normal guy, manipulative, chauvinistic, lazy and terribly messy. But the way he lived his life can help others."

For me, Dan is anything but normal: he is mythic, outsized. His life is like an outline--just enough around the edges to give guidance, with room for me to fill in the details. I see him so clearly in my mind, this person I will never meet--lanky and laughing on a bright white beach, wading through the tepid waters of the Indian Ocean. Alive.

BAHARI, 2006

Dan came into my life ten years ago this month. At the time he had been dead for fifteen years. I was living in Kenya, "teaching English" in a village in the Rift Valley west of Ngong. But I was a terrible teacher with zero training, and I wanted big adventures: I wanted to be Beryl Markham, flying my little two-seater over the Masaai Mara with the savannah spreading out below.

Of course being a bush pilot was pretty much out of the question, but I felt useless and restless in the little village. And so I said my goodbyes. My host mother, Veronica (her Masaai name escapes me now), sent me off with a stunning beaded necklace that I would later hang on the wall of my drab dorm room in the Philadelphia suburbs. I don't remember if I gave her a gift in return. I hope that I did.

Leaving the Rift Valley meant a dusty, hours-long, shoulder-to-shoulder ride in the back of a pickup truck to the nearest town, where one could then catch a van to Nairobi. I think I stayed in Nairobi for a couple of nights and flew to Dar Es Salaam, but I remember arriving in Dar on a bright day in early spring.

The volunteer organization I was working with provided housing just outside Dar, in what we came to call the Bahari Beach House. The house itself was big and airy, with a screened porch and tile floors that were pleasantly cool most of the day. I shared a room with Elsa, a French girl who chain-smoked cigarettes and had big brown eyes. Our room had a bathroom attached and a king bed with a swathe of mosquito netting that we used as a curtain to separate our respective sides. Elsa insisted on sleeping under the net and I hated it, it was hot and unbearable when mosquitos got trapped inside.

We were seven after I arrived at the house. We played a lot of cards because there wasn't much else to do and the sand at midday burned the bottoms of your feet if you walked too far. The sea was tepid like old bathwater and I missed the cold of the Atlantic, but in the evening it was the most beautiful place in the world. The sky was pink and yellow and we swam to keep warm.

We spent our weekdays painting a nearby school whose children were on vacation, and after the children returned we would visit during the day, playing with them and helping out wherever it was needed. For a while we went to the orphanage down the road and helped care for the children until one of the babies got sick and the Catholic mothers didn't want so many people visiting anymore.

During the week we went to work and on weekends we took a taxi into town, usually one driven by a man named Joseph, who smoked Kenyan Portsman cigarettes, as they were called then. Joseph had a big laugh and eventually a daughter named Princess but his car was too small for all of us and everyone had to get out to go over potholes. We made friends with some bush pilots from South Africa. They had good stories and were always having adventures and getting uproariously drunk.

Sometimes Joseph would drive Elsa and me into town and we would meet the Italians. The Italians were older and worked at the embassy and lived in a house by the sea. The two of them would make us dinner with imported pasta and we would sit around on their oriental rugs drinking wine and reading Baudelaire poems. I liked to climb up to their roof to see the stars because they felt very close and I could lie on my back and the cement was cold on my shoulders. The palm trees around the house were very tall and their leaves blocked out some of the sky and made a rustling noise like two hands rubbing together.

Years later when I was back in America Elsa called to tell me the Italians had been in a car accident and one of them had died. They always liked to drive very fast and the roads in Tanzania were bad but no one ever expected them to die. We were young and nothing could happen to us. After we hung up the phone I went and lay down in the grass outside and looked up but the pine trees didn't make noise in the wind and I couldn't imagine that house half emptied of its poetry and song.

NEW YORK, 2016

Lately I haven't been sleeping well. When I first moved to New York I refused to bring anything that wasn't strictly necessary--I was tired of lugging things from place to place, and I hated most of my things anyway. I liked to say that if they'd all somehow wound up in a bonfire, I wouldn't have cared less.

On the list of things I deemed unnecessary was a bed. So I sleep on a grey inflatable mattress from Wal-Mart, the kind that you keep in the closet for when relatives visit. It's plenty comfortable really, and makes it easy to turn my bedroom into an extra living room for parties (which we've done precisely once, though it's nice to have the option). But the first week one of the panels on the bed blew out and I woke up on the floor. I went looking for epoxy and fiberglass tape, but the man at the hardware store on the corner didn't seem to speak much English and I couldn't figure out how to mime fiberglass, so I wound up with a repair kit for inflatable pool toys. It cost $7.99. I brought it home and sat cross-legged and patched the panel as best I could.

The fix has held for months, but now it has a tiny hole somewhere that lets out just enough air so I wake up most mornings around four in a soft little dimple in the middle. I can't find the hole to fix it, so I've taken to embracing my new predawn awakeness to re-read the books that I brought with me, the ones I deemed more important than proper furniture. A few have been added to the pile--the stories of John Cheever, which I bought at the used bookstore on 79th street partly because I like Cheever and partly because I like old books that other people have scribbled in. Last week I found a fat biography of Walt Whitman with a note on the title page: *"So you will remember me. --Anna."*

Sometimes I open my laptop, although I hate the neon glare so early in the morning. Today I checked for an answer from Dan's friend Aidan Hartley, who wrote to me last week that he carries around tattered copies of Anna Karenina and the poetry of Byron, and was touched that I had so much loyalty to his book. "I know it was not a great book," he wrote, "but it was important for me to write it the way it was done."

Why do we carry some things, and leave behind others? I remembered the lists in Tim 'O'Brien's Vietnam War novel, *The Things They Carried*: They carried their own lives. They carried strobe lights and responsibility. They carried jungle boots and Dr. Scholl's foot powder. Syrian refugees take cell phones, prayer beads, chargers, good luck charms, shoes, insulin. The men in Vietnam carried love letters, Kodacolor snapshots. I'm not a refugee or a soldier. I bring my books.

When I wrote to my Bahari housemates to ask what they remembered of *The Zanzibar Chest*, I was surprised to find that not everyone had read it, like I'd thought. But of those who had, it had made a similarly strong impression. One girl sent photographs of her handwritten notes on the book from a decade ago--yellowed pages of quotes she carries with her to this day. One I didn't remember, but I liked: *"I look back now and see how foolishly I longed for scars to make me wise."*

All these years later I'm still carrying the book -- and the photo of Dan -- and still reading about war. I pick up Dexter Filkins' book, *The Forever War*, and open it in the middle; it doesn't matter really where I start and where I end. It all feels the same: bullets and confusion and everyone lying to everyone else and everyone hating the Americans being there and a sense of deep and utter hopelessness. It's like 350 pages asking, what are we all doing here? The Iraqis are there because they have to be, because it's their country and they'll pick up the pieces after everything is said and done. But what about everyone else? At one point Filkins meets CIA Mike, who reminds Filkins of himself. "I looked at his haggard face and I wondered why he'd stayed so long, which was the same question my friends asked me."

Why would someone with any other options go to a place where mass burials are so common that they appear orderly? Why would anyone choose a place where people have learned to dig such a perfect trench? And why would these be people whose words and photographs I carry with me?

"Bearing witness is important," Hartley told me, of his time covering war. "It was worth it. You're going to die of something. Those of us who made it through the nineties are now dying of cancer, suicide or boredom."

MOSHI, 2008

The first time I left Africa it was largely for practical reasons. I had been accepted to university in the United States; I'd resisted at first, but there'd never really been a question of my not attending. Besides, Bahari was emptying, all of us drifting back to our respective realities. I loved Tanzania, but I didn't know what I would do if I stayed.

I moved to Philadelphia, first to the leafy suburbs and later to a room in a townhouse in the city, next to a community garden that had a fig tree and a wrought iron table where I liked to sit and read. One of my housemates from Tanzania lived nearby and we become good friends, spending long nights up on his roof, drinking wine and looking out over the city. We dreamed up plans to go back to Africa; we solved the world's problems and watched the sunset.

The following summer I returned to Tanzania--this time to a town at the base of Mount Kilimanjaro--under the auspices of doing research, a project that was constantly close to falling apart. I spent my days visiting orphanages and my nights sitting on curbs, looking for children to interview--the project was on "access to healthcare for street children," but they weren't as easy to identify as I'd imagined.

One afternoon I met a young woman--my age, maybe younger--all bones and skin, so it was hard to tell. She was crying--she'd lost her child to AIDS. She needed money, and a doctor. I went with her and paid for the visit; we went weekly after that. I would wait for her in the stifling waiting room, sitting among the patients on the cool tile floor. Afterwards we would eat Zanzibar Pizza--flaky dough stuffed with minced spiced lamb, vegetables and eggs that crumbled and left your fingers greasy. We sat on white plastic chairs, mostly in silence. Her English was fair and my Swahili passable, but our conversations were stilted--whether she enjoyed my company or simply felt obligated I could never tell.

In Moshi I fell in kid-love with the DJ at a local club. His name was Goodluck--although everyone called him DJ, which he hated, and I called him Goody--and the club was outside of town in a dusty field. I liked to go midweek, when they played mostly Tanzanian music. He drank dark frothy Guinness--a luxury in Moshi. Goody taught me to dance like a Tanzanian--a slow, foot-to-foot shuffle, a little bob of the shoulders. Sometimes he would let me put on his clunky headphones and teach me to scratch, but I could never get the rhythm quite right. We had careless fun. We stayed out all night and danced down the street in the shimmery hours of the early morning.

One night Goody took me to a corner of town I didn't know, what felt like an endless piki piki ride down dusky winding streets. Piki pikis are motorbikes--small things, 150 CCs or less. It was a dark night and the room we entered was darker--layers of shadows. When my eyes adjusted I saw a man, his ribs protruding under a thin t-shirt, lying in the corner on a dingy mattress. He didn't say anything to me. The air inside felt damp and warm and full of sickness. I don't remember much else; whether Goody explained what was happening, or where we were. I'm sure he did. He was thoughtful in that way.

The next day we had lunch, and Goody asked me for money. He didn't need much, he explained, and it was for his uncle--the man I'd met--who was dying of AIDS. Everyone was dying of AIDS.

We'd been holding hands across the table; I let go and leaned back. A space opened between us. He made good money at his job, and had never asked me for anything.

I gave him the money; I had it, and I cared for him. But everything had shifted. Everything felt unsteady.

ON LEAVING, 2008

I don't remember the day I left Africa for the second time. I don't remember packing my room, or my suitcase, or saying goodbye to friends, although I'm sure I did all of those things. But I remember the ten hour bus ride to Nairobi: opening the windows even an inch invited a thick coating of red dust on everything, so we kept them closed, sweat soaking between shoulder blades and pooling under thighs. Two seats in the back were inexplicably missing, literally ripped from their posts; I assumed they'd been bounced out at some point on the roads, which washed away each year in the spring rains.

I remember hours into the ride the woman across the aisle pulled back her bright khanga to reveal a sleeping baby. The baby was so still and quiet it looked nearly dead. African children rarely cried--there are actually whole articles written on this, associating it with breastfeeding frequency--which this woman began to do, using her free hand to reach across and pull her dress aside. The child stirred and latched on; she covered its head with the cloth, leaned back and closed her eyes. I watched them for a while--the shifting bundle, the tired mother. The desert ricocheted past the windows and darkness fell.

Goody came with me, even though he had a bad back and the bus ride was nearly torture. He never complained, but held my hand and napped in spurts. Sometimes he would wake up and ask if I would consider staying. I couldn't, I would answer--I had to go home, finish school, do the things that were expected of me--although it wasn't strictly true. Of course I could have stayed, if I'd really wanted to. I loved Africa. It felt expansive, big enough to hold all of my fantasies, enough for a whole life of madcap adventures in untamed places. But there were so many other roads to wander down--and I knew that while I might visit again it was unlikely I would stay. I was dreaming of the north, the patterned mosaics of mosques in Marrakech, the murky waters of the Nile. Or maybe south or west--see the bright beaches of Madagascar, the thick green jungles of Congo.

The central bus terminal in Nairobi is a lawless dirt lot in the middle of the city. Vendors push mesh bags of green-skinned oranges through bus windows, skinny boys in torn flip-flops hawk bottled water and candy. We arrived in the warm misty hours just before dawn. I know we ate lavishly and slept well and took a taxi to the airport the next morning. I remember waving as I passed through the security scanner--but Goody was already walking away, back turned, ambling toward the matatu stand with his tired swagger.

As a reporter, I talk to a lot of people. I speak to them in coffee shops, on the street, at community meetings. I call strangers halfway around the world and ask them personal, potentially invasive questions (nicely, of course). This story was no different. Dan had a family that survived him: a mother and father, a sister with whom he was close. I had been following the work of his mother and sister for years; they run a foundation inspired by Dan and his life. When I began to write this story I wrote them a rambling note explaining what I was doing, asking if they would be willing to speak to me. Dan's mother Kathy replied within days. She left me a kind voicemail agreeing to be interviewed, with the best number to reach her.

I never called. I thought about it; more than once I picked up the phone and dialed. Weeks passed. I got sick, then I got better; I wrote more and contacted other people involved in the story. I felt guilty. I thought about what I might say to Kathy--how to convey the weight of her son's life in my own, how to offer my condolences for a tragedy that happened nearly a quarter century earlier. How to tell her that I simply wasn't ready--am not ready--to bring Dan to life. He exists for me in this photograph, in his journals, in the memories of his friends--and that, for now, is enough.

In the decade since I left Goody at the airport in Nairobi I have lived in two dorm rooms, a townhouse, two cabins, a horse barn, a tent, three apartments and a sailboat. Most of these spaces have been furnished, which means spending my days among other people's things--drinking coffee from the retired couple's vintage Fiesta ware, pulling the engineer's wool blankets around me in the winter, setting the table with the dishes of the traveling physician. I don't mind this at all. I like stepping in and out of the lives of others. I like seeing all the ways there are to live in this world.

I'd like to think this is something Dan and I have in common, Dan whose photograph and story are some of the few constants in my life. Dan visited dozens of countries and traveled thousands of miles before he died at 22. The beginning of the quote scribbled on the photo has been left off, but it's important: *Mission of Safari as a Way of Life*. In Kiswahili, *safari* means journey; a derivative of the Arabic سفر, or *safar*, to travel--travel as a way of life. Journey as a way of life.

- - -

KATE COUGH is a journalist who likes stories of all kinds. You can find her other work at kaitlincough.com.

POSTSCRIPT

The conceit of the Memory Project was to tell a story based on a photo. I knew immediately the one I would use: the only photo on the bare walls of my apartment, a photo of a man I've never met, who died when I was a child. The photo was a gift, and for years I have carried it with me, along with a torn copy of Aidan Hartley's The Zanzibar Chest.

I re-read my journals, I contacted old friends and Hartley himself; I combed through the news reports of Dan's death. In some cases my memory was wrong, or shaky-- the journals helped correct things, as did my friends.

I didn't find it odd that I carried around this photo-- I didn't think about it at all really. I just carried it. It wasn't until my editor asked the question that I really considered it. Why do I carry around a photo of a man I've never met-- a man I will never meet, who died before I was born?

10 Rooms With a View

Remembering my Damascus, the city I cannot return to.

By Sarah Dadouch

The day before I missed my plane back home and got stuck in California for a week, I received an email from my father. The subject line read, "The view from my window last week made me think of you." The email itself consisted of an attached photo taken from our apartment's balcony in Damascus. It showed the big park across from my building, covered in snow, the trees leaning sideways from its weight. It was the first Damascus winter I'd missed and as I stared at the photo, I realized I had never seen that much white covering my usually warm city. My family was enjoying the biggest snowfall the city had seen in 30 years, while I stared at a screenshot halfway across the world, the California sun shining outside my window as it always does.

The next day I missed my flight. I went back home for three days, cried myself to sleep every day and cried when I woke up and realized I was still not home. All my friends had left for break, my $300 laptop from Best Buy broke and died on me, and my red flip-phone had no internet capabilities. I read four books and ate fried chicken sandwiches in bed. I went back to the airport extra early to catch my make-up flight. "We can't put you on the flight," the woman at the airport desk snapped at me. "There's a snowstorm in Europe and everything is canceled."

I went back to the dorms and spent four more days reading books and eating fried chicken sandwiches in bed. My suitcases remained unpacked. When I went back to the San Francisco airport for the third time, they told me I could get on the plane. I was ecstatic when I landed in Paris, less ecstatic when I saw everyone stuck and camped out in Charles De Gaulle, everyone in desperate need of showers, everyone yelling at the desk attendants, at their phones, at each other. I was ecstatic again when I realized mine was not one of the flights delayed. I got on the flight, ready to take off—and sat on that flight for six hours, still on the tarmac. I had missed my connecting flight from Jordan to Damascus. I borrowed a phone from a nice French man and texted my father before the air hostess barked at us to turn off our phones. I sat down and ignored the Jordanian man next to me telling me he can't believe I'm Syrian because of my blue eyes. I stared out the window when we finally took off, and blanked at what I would do when we landed.

"Sarah Dadouch, report to airport security," the pilot said once we landed in Amman. I stood up, alongside another man whose name they'd called, and walked slowly to the front of the plane, all the other passengers staring at me walk by, wondering what I'd done to have them ask everyone to wait until I disembarked first. The other man whose name they'd called was taken to an interrogation room; I was handed a plane ticket to Damascus for tomorrow and waved through security lines. "Your father called the airport," the gruff Jordanian airport security officer said.

A woman named Claudia picked me up and said she was related to us somehow. My flight back home was the next day at 6 p.m., she told me. It was midnight. I lay in her guest room bed until 6 a.m., pretending to have fallen asleep but actually reading old Arabic fashion magazines about celebrities I'd never heard of and occasionally crying from exhaustion.

When I heard her get up and open and close cabinets in the kitchen at 7 a.m., I got up and joined her. Yes, I slept great, I smiled. Thank you for having me, but I'm not waiting 11 hours for a flight. I'm taking a cab.

She tried to talk me out of it but I had made up my stubborn 18-year-old mind. I didn't have enough money, but she convinced the cab driver that I'd pay him when I got home. "She's from a good family, they'll pay you, I promise," she told him. The man grunted okay, threw out his cigarette, and opened the cab door for me. He chain-smoked the whole drive from Jordan's capital to Syria's capital, and I cried the whole way in the back seat. Quietly, but I'm sure he knew anyway.

Five hours later, I was somewhere outside of Damascus and could see my sister from far away, a tiny dot getting bigger and bigger as she ran towards me and I ran towards her. We slammed into each other, crying and hugging. My mom paid the driver and drove me home.

For four days, I couldn't sleep. I developed a pattern: around 4 a.m. I would give up completely on my bed and move to the living room. I'd try watching old reruns of Friends on the Saudi channel MBC4 for a bit, then go out to the balcony where my father took the snow picture and stand in the crisp December air. I'd watch the sole old man make his way around the park to go to the mosque for dawn prayers and would wonder what he'd do if I yelled out to him into the darkness. I'd watch as dots of light appeared, slowly at first, then almost in unison, as people got up to pray, then all of them turning off lazily as people got back to bed. I'd watch Qasyoon, the big mountain that towers over my city and takes up most of our balcony's view, turn colors: drenched in the cold blue of night first and then fading into pinks and reds as the sun comes up. Then around 7 o'clock, when everyone is starting to wake up and the constant thrum of car horns begins its shouting, I'd go back to the couch and fall asleep, covering myself with my mother's short white wool blanket that we were forbidden from using as kids.

I still have the white wool blanket in my father's house in Austin, Texas, where he lives now. It's in a broken orange carry-on suitcase my mother gave me as a gift when I was 18 and moving to America. The suitcase also has a photo album and a notebook I had in high school. These are most of the things I still have left with me from home: I lost the watch my father had gifted me for my last birthday in Damascus, left it in some restaurant in Berkeley. I lost the turquoise and gold necklace I'd had since I was child in the move after college. I broke all the mugs I had brought with me and can't find any clothes from that time anywhere. But I didn't bring that much stuff with me here in the first place, because I always thought I was going back.

I don't remember the last time I stood on our balcony and stared at the familiar massive mountain staring back at me. I didn't know it was the last time and so it was just a normal day looking out at the view I thought I'd be back to see in a few months. I didn't pack my favorite dress that I wore to my father's engagement party and I didn't pack my Harry Potter copies that had lost their covers and spines from wear. I didn't hug my cousins and aunts and uncle extra hard. I didn't take a photo of my blue and cream bedroom, the colors my father picked because I had told him of a blue and cream room that I read about in a book once. I didn't take a photo of me in my favorite place on earth, the Umayyad Mosque in Old Damascus.

I can Google it in New York now and read in English the things I knew in Arabic: the mosque is 1,383 years old. It was built in 638 on the site of a Christian basilica. It is said that the basilica used to hold the head of John the Baptist, and today it holds Saladin's tomb outside in the courtyard. Before it was a basilica it was a Roman temple.

Outside the mosque is Al Hamidiyeh, my city's famous outdoor *souq*. Google Images can show you photos of its cobblestone streets bustling with people maneuvering between the shops, the *souq*'s very high ceiling peppered with holes to allow streams of light shining down on people like spotlights. But I remember the *souq* at night, when I could hear my heels clicking on the old cobblestones, the sound reverberating across the empty dark streets, the shops' wooden doors bolted shut. My father, sister and I made our way to an old Damascene house where we sat in the courtyard's balcony, drinking tea and listening to a famous Syrian singer's nostalgic Arabic and Armenian songs.

UNESCO's site will tell you that the Ancient City of Damascus, which includes both the mosque and *souq*, is protected as a World Heritage Site. So was the Ancient City of Aleppo with its own Umayyad Mosque, but unlike their counterparts in the capital, the *souq* in Aleppo watched itself burn in fire and the mosque saw its walls, prayer hall, and great gate destroyed and damaged by rocket-propelled grenades. You can find photos of them before the destruction both online and in my father's laptop photo album, when he took us to visit the city back when we were too young to remember. There's a yellowish discolored photo of my grandfather and grandmother smiling politely in the courtyard of Aleppo's mosque, another of my little brother and sister running in the distance down big blocks of steps in the citadel, my other sister kneeling over ahead of them, either staring at something she found in the ancient ground or out of breath.

If you visit the Metropolitan Museum of Art in New York, in the Department of Ancient Near Eastern Art, you can find limestone sculptures from Palmyra in glass boxes with tags next to them that tell their whole history. When I used to go to Tadmur, as we call the ancient city, my father would point at gaps and tell us that the missing sculptures were in famous museums abroad. I didn't quite believe him until I saw the bust of Habba in the Louvre, the 3rd century sculpture's hand weaving through her veil, looking like a girl nervously combing through her hair, who was then unknowingly suspended forever in time. My sister snapped a photo on her iPhone of me by Habba's side, mimicking her movement, and we laughed and moved on, not mentioning the sadness that welled up inside us.

My cousin visited Damascus last summer for the first time in years. He told me he went to our house and took photos. Send them to me, I said. No, he said. I'm worried you'll get too sad. When he finally sent them, I studied them to see the changes in every room: the photos of my cousin and his wife, who had moved in, hung over the fireplace. The new little plant next to the couch, the knick-knacks atop the piano, the fake yellow flowers on the glass kitchen table that my father had emblazoned with quotes from us. My bedroom had changed the most. It had a new dresser and a changing station with baby pictures on the wall adjacent to the one that had hand-written messages from my close friends and family members, saying goodbye before I left the first time. The books I had left behind were now mixed with the ones my father had left, lined up in the living room bookcase. But the balcony view was the same: the houses were intact and the park was still lush with greenery and the mountain was still imposing. The flag I once considered my own is flying in the distance, right next to where the sun was setting when my cousin took the photo.

I saw the photo and looked at the view in my New York dorm room: the Hudson right next door and New Jersey in the distance. It's beautiful, just like the view from my apartment in the Turkish border town of Gaziantep, overlooking the busy street leading to the Old City where men with motorcycles yelled in Turkish and where my vegetable guy whistled every morning as he arranged his batches of parsley and mint. My view in Istanbul before that was of an endless sea of fir trees, sometimes topped with caps of snow, covering the graveyard we lived next to, with houses beyond that as far as I could see. My Berkeley apartment's view was less exciting, overlooking the daycare below us and the children who woke me up each morning with their squealing and their scampering.

My father packed up most of his life in suitcases and said a halfhearted goodbye to the apartment he had been working on all my life. He had a return ticket booked, thought he would be back in three months, did not anticipate the bombing that kept him away. But he took one last glance at the living room as he left, knowing he was officially, for now, moving out. He saw his black and white photographs that he had printed and framed and hung on the living room wall, the very very very old green and beige fabric duck that sat on the couch's arm and had a torn pouch that was meant to hold the TV remotes, the gardenia tree that always threatened to die but always came through with blossoms, and the line of weird trees whose seeds my dad smuggled in from outside the country that grew inside the house and gave the living room a permanent jungle feel.

It is said that when the Prophet Mohammad got to the borders of Damascus, he stopped and said, "man should only enter paradise once, and I choose the one above." And so he sat down, stared at my city from afar, got his full of it, then got up and continued on his way.

I sat on that balcony most days of my life, eating cheese sandwiches and watermelon slices in the heat and drinking tea and hot cocoa in the cold. I stared at my city and was never tired of it staring back. I picked the gardenia flowers and let them float in bowls of water, like my mother taught me, their aroma lingering in whatever room I placed them in. My sister and I chased our turtle around on that balcony, until it died. We chewed massive amounts of gum and stuck them onto cracks that leaked out ants, thinking we were solving the problem. I met my stepmother on that balcony, her nervously showing up with gifts for the oldest daughter she'd heard a lot about. We took a bad, blotchy family photo there the night of my father's engagement, one of those monstrosities in which everyone either looks bloated or has his eyes closed. And that is one of the few photos I have on that balcony, because we never took photos of our ordinary everyday life in Damascus.

I don't remember what I did and where I went the last time I was in my city. I don't remember the last meal I ate or the last thing I saw. I don't remember whether I overslept the morning I left or if I woke up early to catch my flight. I don't remember crying. I don't remember what I left behind because I left behind so much. I didn't put my memories in a suitcase or document them in photographs because I thought I was coming back and packing memories and taking photos happens when you know you're saying goodbye.

A few months after I left, I sat in the right back seat of my father's car in a border town in Texas, watching the sparse greenery zoom by, deformed by the speed. "We are not going back home," my father told me. I looked at his face in the rearview mirror. He pretended to be focused on the road but really he doesn't like to look you in the eye when he tells you something serious. "We can't go back home for a while, not until Assad is gone or things change."

I don't remember crying. I remember my sister being next to me in the backseat but I remembered wrong: she was still in Syria. We don't cry about missing home because ours is still intact and our family is still alive whereas so many others have had their favorite balconies and bedrooms blown off and have watched their families die in their arms or burn in front of them or foam at the mouth from chemical weapons being dropped on their beloved cities.

Instead, my sister and I cried during a trailer once while waiting for a comedy to start and she just turned to me and pointed at her face and said, "I don't know why."

We talk about home without crying, about the open-faced cheese pastries, the oil-pickled eggplants, the juicy apples and grapes. We talk about the smells of jasmine mixed with the smells of sewers, the smell of hairspray mixed with cigarette smoke.

We talk about the happy things and the ugly things. How judgmental everyone was, how generous everyone was. How our grandma was a bad cook but because we lived on the floor above we ate her food most days of the week, but how her grape leaves and kibbeh are the best in the world—and how she could order in Syrian food like no other.

If we wanted to cry, we would do it separately, by talking about the small things. I would say, remember that cabinet in my room with the book shelves on top? I wonder if my books and teddy bears are still there. And she would say, yeah that's the cabinet I cried on when I found out Fred died in Harry Potter.

She would say, remember when you'd mess up dad's espresso because you were 12 and couldn't concentrate to save your life? And I would say, remember how you used to get so mad at me and so I would make milkshakes and put them outside your door as an apology? Remember our red bunk beds, she would say.

Remember when you fell at Krak de Chevaliers because dad told you to tie your shoes and you didn't and so you split your head open and I held your bloody face and hair in my 6-year-old hands, praying to god all the way back home that you wouldn't die, I would say.

Remember Grandma's yellow house where we spent all our summers and how we boiled tomatoes for weeks and it made you hate hot tomatoes forever? she'd say.

I wouldn't tell her, the house whose side was bombed in the town that was under siege for months whose people were starving.

I remember, I'd say.

- - -

SARAH DADOUCH *is a Syrian journalist who covers Syria and Turkey. You can follow her work on Twitter at @SarahDadouch.*

POSTSCRIPT

When I first started writing for this project, I picked a photo of my sister, my cousin and me standing in the open courtyard of the Umayyad Mosque in Damascus, our 7-year-old selves flashing my father wide toothy smiles, focused on the camera's lens and not thinking about how ancient the floor we're standing on is, how much the pillars behind us have seen of history.

But when I started writing, I didn't know where I was going. Many better writers have already written about the mosque. My story was different in that it focused on how this is the one photo I have of one of my favorite places on earth: I went there often and always assumed I would go back, so I didn't take photos every visit. In a pre-iPhone world, taking a photo was more cumbersome: you'd have to remember to pack the camera and buy film and take the photo and take the film to the guy to develop and remember to buy a photo album and remember to write on the back of the photo the date of when the photo was taken before slipping it into one of the see-through pockets, where it sits for a long time, occasionally seen when you take out the photo albums at family parties and sit around with your cousins, pointing at weird hairdos and those god-awful bulky patterned sweaters your mother used to dress you in. So we didn't take photos there because we went often and didn't need a photo to remind us of the familiar mosque.

But the more I started to write about this—about the feeling of taking a place for granted and thinking you'll come back before realizing you might never be able to — the more I realized that what I really wanted to write about was not the impressive, old building that is the Umayyad Mosque but a much less famous one: the ordinary-looking building I grew up in across the park. I started writing and realized that I had remembered some things incorrectly, the main thing being that I assumed that, when he left his apartment for the last time, my father had packed his bags with the full knowledge that he would not be coming back soon. As it turns out, he had a return ticket for a couple months later, which he had to cancel. He, like I, did not know his last time in the apartment would be his last.

This story is about one apartment that most readers had never seen and would never see (I say most because I assume my family will be my main audience). I could have chosen one of the photos my cousin took of the apartment when he visited it last year, but I chose instead my favorite photo of the view from our balcony, a place that, when I remember it, feels simultaneously real and imagined, like something out of a familiar movie. Thinking of its gardenia tree brings a swirl of nostalgia that hits my heart so hard it takes me a while to recover. The idea that I may never be able to return is still something I cannot accept.

11 The Girl Who Would Be a Scholar

My grandmother wanted one thing from a husband. School.

By Tony Lin

In 1956, a sixth grade girl uttered the words that launched a lifelong battle between her and her fate.

She said, "I'll marry whoever pays for my school."

And she did.

The girl in this photograph is my grandma, captured when she was 10 years old. She was a fisherman's daughter who lived in a remote village in southern China. She was the youngest of three surviving ones. One of her older brothers went fishing but never came back. Her little brother died of measles when he was only eight.

The family's name was Yang. In Chinese, the character means aspens—the most common trees in the country. The Yangs were like other families in the village: they lived on fresh seafood in the high season, salted fish in off season, and sun-dried sweet potatoes during food shortages, which were most of the time.

For a poor village girl, Grandma's path was supposed to be clear: when she was old enough she would follow her big sister and marry, possibly a nice young peasant from a town nearby who'd offer a decent bride-price to the family. Her parents, though hardly rich, would be generous enough to provide her a piece of gold jewelry—a bracelet, or a pair of earrings—as a wedding gift. Marriage would make her a part of her husband's family. Her value as a daughter to her own family would end.

"A married daughter is like spilled water," goes a rural Chinese saying.

Only once a year, on the third day after the Chinese New Year, would a married daughter be permitted to visit her parents' home bearing gifts.

But Grandma had a different plan.

Her story was *almost* about how school changed a village girl's fate.

At that time, it was almost unheard of for a poor family to send a girl to school, let alone buy her textbooks and stationary. But grandma was lucky: In 1950, the newly established Communist Chinese government began to expand its rural reform and promote education and gender equality. The village cadres went from home to home, mobilizing parents to send children to schools—especially girls. Grandma's older siblings were too old, and her little brother—then alive—was too young. Grandma was then 11 and was the only school-age child in the Yang family.

Her primary school was a big room. It was the largest space in the village, what had been the living room of the home of an overseas businessman. The school taught two courses through first grade to third: Chinese literature and mathematics. All the grades were taught at the same time—while the teacher was teaching the first graders, the older students studied by themselves.

Along with grandma, there were five girls at school at first, but they left one by one—some chose housework over school and some couldn't keep up with the lessons. Some had to leave because their families did not want them in school.

So by third grade Grandma became the only girl in her village classroom. She was smart, diligent, and strategic about finding a middle path between schoolwork and chores. She'd get up in the morning and cook meals for the family. By the end of third grade, she was an A student, and was offered an opportunity to transfer to a better school in the town nearby.

In her new school, she was one of just three girls in a class of 50. Grandma remained a top student, with an almost perfect academic record but for one exception: she had a terrible Mandarin accent.

"I guess I wanted to be a doctor," she recalled decades later. "My family thought maybe I should be a teacher, but my accent was pretty bad and I hate singing and dancing." Most teachers had to teach multiple art subjects at that time.

The principal encouraged her to go to middle school, offering her a precious spot in a middle school 33 miles away. If she went to middle school, she'd live in the dorm and come home once a week.

Her family, however, rejected the opportunity. Her mother, whose family gave her away to her future husband's household when she was a month old, had died of a chronic lung disease. The Yang family was then run by Grandma's brother's wife who thought girls going to middle school was simply ludicrous.

She told Grandma to drop out of school and follow the traditional path to marriage.

Grandma announced, "I'll marry whoever pays for my school."

Her story was *almost* about how a marriage changed a village girl's life.

The word got out quickly: Fisherman Yang's daughter, the beautiful and educated girl, was offering herself in marriage to anyone who would pay for her to stay in middle school.

Word reached the mother of a young welder who had left a nearby village and moved away to Beijing to work on China's space program. The family was well-off: the welder's father, who left home for business in Southeast Asia, mailed money back home every month. His mother was determined that her son marry a local girl.

The mother met a local matchmaker who showed her Grandma's picture. She liked what she saw and sent a message to Grandma expressing the family's interest.

"She sent a photo of him," Grandma later told me. "It was a half-length portrait. He seemed like a decent man."

"Remember," she recalled the matchmaker telling her, "the man's family offered to pay for your tuition. That means, it is okay if he wants to dump you. However, it is not okay if you want to dump him."

Grandma agreed to the match.

It wasn't until after they were officially engaged that Grandma saw a full-length photo of Grandpa. She recalled a photo of him standing in a playground somewhere in Beijing.

"He looked kind of tall," she said.

Finally, two years later, Grandpa returned from Beijing for a short visit. It was the first time Grandma saw him in person—he was not as tall as the photo looked like. But he seemed kind.

They were married on August 1stst, 1958. Grandpa, who had just 12 days for vacation every year, went back to Beijing after the wedding. Grandma, in keeping with the tradition, left her home and moved in with Grandpa's family, which was presided over by his older brother.

Grandpa sent her money every month. And with his financial support, grandma completed middle school and graduated with distinction.

Upon graduation, the teachers sat her down and tried to talk her into high school. They offered her a spot at a renowned municipal high school.

"I was thinking about going to a nursing program," she said. It would be a more stable path than medical school, and she could start making money more quickly. "But the teachers thought I had the potential to be a university student. They really wanted me to continue high school and take the college entrance examination."

She wrote to her husband.

"University? Why not," he replied. "I'll support it as long as you can keep going to school."

So a fisherman's daughter from rural southern China became a high school student in the late 1950s.

In modern China, there are many stories about how rural students made it to a top university against all odds. My grandma's life is not one of those stories.

The pain firstly started in her neck, then spread to her back. It was her first year in high school and she tried to push through it while preparing for the university entrance exam.

Food was scarce and nutrition poor. The Party had food quotas for citizens based on the size of households. Grandma was assigned with 22 pounds of food supplies a month. There were no vegetables or fruits, let alone protein.

The searing neck pain was mixed with stress and malnutrition, which ultimately evolved into neurasthenia, a psychological condition that causes fatigue and anxiety. She couldn't fall asleep at night or focus in the morning. Her memory suffered.

Grandma left school for a year to recover, leaving the dormitory to return to her husband's family. She tried to return to school but the illness persisted.

"I had to say farewell to school," she wrote in her memoir.

As a rural Chinese wife, it was time to be a mother and give birth to a son.

Her ordeal was about to begin.

China's household registration system prohibited Grandma from moving to Beijing to be reunited with Grandpa. She was registered in Fujian and if she did move away she would become a ghost in Beijing's bureaucratic system—a so called "black name." No food quota, no work, and no social status whatsoever.

So Grandma, a high school dropout who dreamed of being a doctor, stayed with her husband's family and found temporary jobs.

My great grandmother didn't say much when Grandma gave birth to her first daughter in 1960s, even though she had not given the family a valued son. She was visibly annoyed, three years later, when the second daughter was born. She cried and screamed, when she found out the third grandchild was female as well. And she ordered Grandma to give the fourth daughter away.

"I asked her if she had to make me do it, please find a nice family for the girl," Grandma recalled. "But the in-law said, 'Good family? She should be thankful that I didn't use her to fish sea cucumbers.'"

In their part of southern China, sea cucumbers were a delicacy, and they were rumored to feed on human flesh. A prevailing urban myth was that families use undesired female infants as bait to fish for sea cucumbers.

Grandma was reduced to tears. She says she cried so much that even now, a half century later, her eyes still hurt every time she cries.

But Grandpa was not upset. "Four daughters," he told his mother. "So what? I'll take them all!"

Grandpa would not let his youngest daughter be given away. But he couldn't protect Grandma from being bullied by his family. Finally, in 1971, 13 years after they were married, Grandma moved illegally to Beijing with their four daughters—adding five "black names" to Grandpa's one-person food quota. Their living situation would not improve until the 1980s.

So this would not be one of those stories about a rural woman's epic achievement during China's economic reform, where adventurers made fortunes when they ventured into a bourgeoning market.

But it *almost* is.

It takes a particular set of skills to support six people on a one person's budget in one of the bleakest eras in modern China – the last years of the Cultural Revolution. Grandma adapted. She learned a skill – candling eggs: determining the quality of eggs by holding them up to a candle light. She learned how to make ketchup from raw tomatoes (better and cheaper!). And to accommodate her daughters' growth she learned how to sew, lengthening their dresses, and eventually making their clothes.

"People thought we were rich," my aunt, Lin Wen, the third daughter, told me. "But we are not even registered in Beijing."

Her skills improved so much that Grandma's underground tailoring business expanded from doing "favors" in exchange for food in the 1970s, to beginning to charge in the less restrictive 1980s. Men began needing suits for their interactions with foreigners and Grandma, now known as Tailor Yang, was made some of the best around. In time she had to hire apprentices and train her daughters to keep up with the workload.

By now Grandma, who was in her late 30s, was making twice as much as her engineer husband.

The story would've been an inspiring business case study if Grandma had not had to close her business in 1989. Her oldest daughter—then a graduate student at a top university—had gotten pregnant by mistake.

"I told her don't have the abortion, and don't quit school either," Grandma said. "If you can't raise the child at the moment, I'll do it."

And so she did.

The birth of her first grandchildren marked the end of her professional pursuit. She didn't have to worry about candling eggs and making ketchup. But she did make clothes for the child.

Then came another grandchild, followed by two more. Grandma spent the next almost 20 years helping to take care of all her grandchildren, all the way through college.

Grandpa died from a stroke in 2010, two years after their 50th anniversary – and 52 years after Grandma vowed to marry a man who would pay for school. She now lives alone in an apartment that the government gave to Grandpa. She finally has a household registration in Beijing, as well as a governmental allowance.

Two of her four daughters have become successful in Fujian, one as a professor and the other a stock broker. And the other two daughters, though not as professionally successful, visit her three times a week.

The only argument the daughters occasionally have with her is whether Grandma should move back to Fujian. The successful daughters want to be closer to her, where they can provide for a better life.

"No," she'd vocally object at first, giving some vague excuses. But recently she just ignores the proposal altogether.

The daughters don't quite understand her decision: why not move back to her hometown, where she understands the dialect and knows many more people?

Grandma, as a rural woman in southern China, spent most of her years in search for freedom, and she missed the shot almost every time.

She had almost been a university student. She had almost been a doctor. She had almost become a successful businesswoman.

The only certainty in her life, at the age of 80, is the life living in her own apartment left by her husband.

She is free, finally. She has what she always wanted.

TONY LIN *is a professional procrastinator with side jobs like writing and filmmaking. His work has appeared in Washington Post, The Economist, GLAAD and various outlets. Follow him at medium.com/@tony_lin*

The Memory Project

PRIX RTL GRAND PUBLIC 82

DEUX CENTS LECTEURS ONT ÉLU
"RETOUR A MALAVEIL"
DE CLAUDE COURCHAY

● Lauréat du Prix RTL
Grand Public, Claude Courchay
pour "Retour à Malaveil"
(Ed. du Seuil), c'est dans sa
grande tradition que le jury,
composé de 200 lecteurs
sélectionnés sur LIPOS,
s'est prononcé pour les
ouvrages à qui des plus
beaux, mon hoste, auxquels
jusqu'à l'amitié continuait à
l'appréci.

Le roman de Claude
Courchay raconte le retour
d'un ancien dans son...

village dans les Cévennes,
Claude revient, alors, que
se décide de non et
religieuxà à Malaveil...
au silence son de partie,
Noël Blanc « est le temps de
l'hésitage, qui ne soit » de
sent « qui se a été,
endeuil la responsabilité
d'un crime auteur qu'il y a
pas eu envie. Mais "Retour
à Malaveil" n'est pas
seulement le récit d'une
vengeance, c'est aussi un
livre tout de tendresse et de
douleur.

Claude Courchay, 49 ans,
été à la fois moraliste et
journaliste. Il a déjà publié
huit romans dont aucun
n'avait rencontré un public
avant "Retour à Malaveil".
l'éclate un jury donc, réalisé
grâce au Prix RTL Grand
Public. Claude Courchay
pourra aller à côté Rachel,
Daniel B', et raconté une
cérémonie qui présidaient
que Jean-Jacques Pauvert,
Président Jacques
Laurentin, Solange
Fasquelle, Roger Continente
et René Julliet. ■

Réunis dans le Grand Studio de RTL à l'occasion de la remise du Prix (de g. à d.) : Pierre Bellfond, l'éditeur Jacques Bignod,
Président de RTL : Claude Courchay, lauréat 82 ; Jean-Jk Jolly, ancien lauréat, Raymond Castans, Directeur des Programmes de RTL,
Guy Berlier, lauréat 81...

"A savoir "Retour à Malaveil", j'ai
déjà écrit cette l'histoire d'autant que si
n'aborde ce se de si est mais savoir,
admettre, Claude Courchay ain...

12 Fragments From My Father

He lives in a remote farmhouse. Sometimes he answers when I call.

By Diego Courchay

"The problem, is living. Yes? To sneak through that fine margin between boredom and fear. To find a lifeline that isn't a fugue."

Claude Courchay.

It cost me seven dollars to buy this picture of my father. It's a bargain, a 1982 antique listed in Italian on eBay by a French seller. Fifteen days for shipping.

I discovered it online. Only moments before, he was distant, but then, on the screen, my father is all smiles. Daddy's having a good day: arms confidently crossed, in laid-back attire, listening to something being said just out of view as he's surrounded by four men in suits, all there for him. This is as good as it gets. There's a movie deal on the way, he's living in Paris, and just last year the Left he voted for won the French presidency for the first time.

I turn to the next page and he turns towards me and I see his face up close. He's only 49, all grizzly beard and long hair, still barely greying, still without the hole underneath his left eye where the tumor will be surgically removed.

For now, his ninth book, a novel, has brought him critical acclaim. This I learn reading the review that accompanies the photos I've just bought. It's a two-page spread on yellowing paper, "200 readers have chosen *Retour à Malaveil* by Claude Courchay." The photo on the left shows the presentation of the 1982 RTL prize for literature, the one on the right his portrait in full.

My father was born in 1933. He has never so much as turned on a computer, yet the ways of the Internet are inscrutable and will include even those who resist it: *pausito83*, a seller on the Italian version of eBay, lists this fragment of his past. I write to ask where he found it and a woman named

Christine replies that it's from the weekly *Paris-Match*. She wishes my family and I all the best, and an *eccellente giornata*.

At some point before this story is published he'll go to see his mentor, Simone de Beauvoir, and ask her, "Did you think I would make it?"

"No," she'll reply.

She had once told him, "You're in full possession of all your defects."

From here on, the legend goes, he'll stop being a struggling journalist. He'll buy a house in the city, another in the country and a new car. That's the way he tells it "That book took me out of the streets." Later on, he'll indulge in other things he no longer expected — a third marriage, even a son. This only happens six years later, after he meets a woman 25 years his junior while reading in a cemetery.

There's a single quote by him, right beneath the portrait on the second page. "Through *Retour à Malaveil* I may have written the love story I never lived with my mother." She died in 1968, a widow at an early age who brought up three children during World War Two. The novel is about the war. The review says it's about man framed for murder who returns home after 15 years in prison. It's about what happened during the war, what happened right after, and the things people did to each other.

The novel ends with a father and a son who never met buried in the same grave, a lifetime apart. My father lost his father when he was five, to alcoholism and malaria. He has a single memory of him. I have more. They've cost me, though this is the first time I pay for one.

It's been 10 months since we've talked. I see him smiling in 1982. He's 83 years old now and says never been happier. And I believe him.

"It doesn't work. It can never work. Us schizos roam around in our shell. That's the burden. An accompanied schizo is just a schizo dreaming of being alone."

Claude Courchay

He'll only tell me about the past when I visit him in the house on the hill where he lives alone. On those evenings there'll be cards and wine, then maybe rum or Jack Daniels. Every so often I'll step outside to smoke. You'll hear a deer bark if it's mating season, cicadas in the summer, but usually it's just two voices with not another soul for miles. When I can't go visit, contact is scarce, though I've never gone so long without hearing his voice.

He used to write; I never answered. We've mostly lived on different continents and he'd send postcards — at first full of drawings for a child too young to read, then letters I'd decipher, on white notepad from a French publisher, with red edges and book titles in the bottom left corner. When he travelled there were photographs and exotic stamps, from Australia, Hong Kong, New York, Mongolia. Later on he sent me articles and cartoons cut from newspapers, on whatever he read that brought me to mind; they had me reading news for the first time. I never got around to writing back. It was always one-way traffic until the summers when I crossed the Atlantic.

Now the one-sidedness is all mine. His aversion to technology means computers, cellphones, the Internet itself, and all that interconnectivity from Facebook, to Whatsapp, to Skype has never reached his hilltop. There's an old telephone, for what it's worth. Their relationship is complicated. He'll tolerate its existence, as long as it doesn't ring. When it does he'll loudly curse its intrusion, and sullenly ignore it. The ringing of the phone is emotional blackmail: never give in, never pick up. "It makes it hard to reach you," I once ventured, knowing that was the point. We had system in place for years, where I'd call and let it ring three times, hang up and call again so he'd know it was me. That implied a lot of obnoxious sound but at least he could be sure it wasn't a trap, a salesman, an old acquaintance, or whatever else the world threatens to offer him. That stopped working last summer. I've varied the number of calls — three, four, five times, three rings, vainly trying to crack the code of his distrust. So I leave a message on the answering machine about once a month. I know he hears them, standing by the piano he uses as a table, nodding to himself before returning to reading or writing a book.

I have that image in my mind's eye; I have the photograph purchased on eBay. They're the two extremes of a life fleeing the middle ground, with one man beyond reach on an island of his own making, and the other, the perennial "fuck up," belatedly earning the jackpot of fame and recognition. The explanation for both is half a century in the making, and it reads like a history book thrown into a mixer: when you're born the year Hitler came to power, you get the stutters, he'd explain. The historical stutters. You're born into a crack in time, a place where anything can happen, and history itself doubts which way it's going, it *stutters*, trying to finish the phrase with everyone holding their breaths to see what it'll end up saying. And when you're born into that, he'd explain, you get a feeling for it, like someone born in a leap year, chasing eclipses all life long. It makes sense then, to be a soldier and a mason, a waiter and a flight attendant, a teacher and a drifter, and to settle for being a journalist and writer getting paid for chasing those stuttering cracks that must feel like home.

But I was born when it was all done and dusted, and history, to him, had run its course. And at the end of times there was silence, sometimes interrupted by the ringing of a phone.

Fighting? So be it. Start with YOUR OWN liberation. Just words. You're getting all worked up, little brother. Life isn't talked, it's walked. Your only chance is a kick in the ass. Who cares for your ass? Still, you can't keep on pretending.

Claude Courchay

When in doubt, look to the mirror to find your father. Mother says so, and she ought to know, as so many mothers who one day exclaimed, "How you look like your father!" His sister said so too, Aunt Maryline, who died years ago. Maybe it's in the cheeks, the shape of the face, the half-smile. In my mother's room there's a photo that could be of me, were it not black and white, taken at some point in the late 1940s — a boy sitting in briefs and short sleeves lifting a baby to its feet with raised arms: her ex-husband and me, the same kid hitting puberty 55 years apart. There's no photo of him at 28; my face today is somewhere in my father's past, somewhere in 1961. Now I have a new photo on the way, him at 49, something to inform my future.

The photograph I bought online arrived in New York in a brown envelope. It was sent by a man named Didier Vancoillie, from a place with the long address of J.J. Bousquet Campinus, at Route Privée Bouverie, in the town Roquebrune-sur-Argens, somewhere in the southeast of France. Google tells me it's a camping site, with a snack-pizzeria and a pool. "Only 7 km from the beach of fine sand." Someone there has kept the cutout of my father's literary breakthrough for 35 years. The French postal service is feeling romantic "Love always finds a way," reads the stamp on the corner of the envelope, next to "Fragile do not bend please." I've called the camping to ask, but no luck so far.

The two pages are carefully cut, protected by a white piece of paper between them. I lay them on the bed and look. There's the article on the left, his portrait on the right. The idea is that images can speak to you. Just look at them long enough to annul and rediscover them, tear them down and put them back together with your eyes. Maybe walk out of the room, pretend you're going to the kitchen and quickly turn back, walk in on them as they're telling their secret. It actually works. I did it once. There was a photo I had looked at from time to time, for five years, copied from a newspaper's webpage onto my desktop, observed and deleted and reclaimed at a later date. It shows a white van, a Ford Expedition Max 2007 in a ditch, awkwardly tilted. Upon closer inspection, the van's roof is sunk in and its hood bent, as if rumpled by a giant fist. There are two firemen in the foreground I willfully ignored every time I tried to see beyond their shiny helmets and coats, at what was left after the crash, the carcass of the van captured by photographers for the next day's edition. Then one day, five years in, I realized what the firemen were there for. The bodies were still inside.

That's what springs to mind, thinking about thinking about a picture of my father on my bed. I called after that crash in 2007, to tell him about the girl inside I knew. He said, "Have a drink." Then, a year later, when I visited him, he said, "me too." It had happened to him in 1968, his first wife and also a car crash. "She was a terrible driver." His mother had also just died. He was living on the island of Guadeloupe; the postal service was delayed by the student protests and he got both letters, for his wife, for his mother, in the same batch.

That brought us together. Then, some months later, I was expelled during my third year in college after consistently drifting, and I visited him again. He said, "me too." From the teacher's training college, in the early 1950's. I was his son after all. He had aged somewhat, after his tumor was extracted and his face bore the mark. It had been a long year and he shared this piece of philosophy: "Life is a series of kicks in the ass until you land where you're supposed to be." He said so with his dry humor, the kind that can weather a storm and come out just as crisp, but rarely allows the company of a smile, or maybe just a half-smile, the raising of the upper lip like on the portrait I'm looking at.

I smile like that too. We both have a crooked lower tooth that can shoulder some of the blame, though I might have modeled it after him. What's inherited and what's copied? What are the chances of losing and failing the same way? What's mimed and what's fate? My father was proud of me. I was kicked out of college and he told me "It's the best thing that's ever happened to you." Welcome off the beaten path, my child. Before that, I'd been too much in the sun, and I don't mean the childhood in California and Mexico. Too tall, for his stunted growth during the war; too handsome, for his ugly duckling persona; too bourgeois for the son of a proud proletarian; too adapted, too well behaved, altogether loveable but foreign and living abroad under another nationality. But it was a matter of time, a bit of symmetry: I was his son after all.

It's all faded a bit since then. Tension followed by release, the elastic that brings you together retracts as distance takes its toll again. Then you find this photo and you wonder about all the things you should be asking, if only ringing phones also meant answering. He's 83 and counting, tick-tock. And there's also that strange idea, after the parallels and common choices, that if you understand his life you'll get a glimpse into what's coming for you, and between both of you, and maybe something can be done about all that.

"The fugue, constant of constants. Rambling around. The essential is to flee. You idiot. Elsewhere it will be the same: you bring yourself along. So what? One day, you'll manage to unhook him."

Claude Courchay

The man in the photo has no imagination. That man receiving a literary prize couldn't think up a story unless he'd put himself through it. At least that's what he used to say, back when he was a journalist, what his best friend from that time repeats to me when we talk on the phone. They did it all together—from the civil war in El Salvador in 1983 to Albania after the fall of the USSR in 1991, to Britain's handover of Hong Kong to China in 1997. Then fifteen years ago they had an argument. "He's really very particular," this friend tells me about the man he crisscrossed the world with, and never spoke to again.

I find photojournalist Michel Setboun after going down a list of the people that could fill in the blanks. Who's still alive who had been close enough back then? I remembered my father's postcards, the anecdotes from faraway places and the name that always accompanied them. It doesn't take long to find Setboun's webpage, and in it all the trips I heard of as a child. There's Tirana right after the end of Communism, and portraits of Salvadorian soldiers, and also all the places they no longer visited together. I scroll through the images, remembering scenes my father had mentioned in passing, hoping he'll appear in the next click alongside some Soviet building. Finally, I use the search icon on the website and his name appears alongside two photographs.

The first shows a soldier in a green uniform with a cap on, half crouching behind the front of a bus, his rifle held up in his left hand, his head twisted back looking at someone to whom he extends his right hand. The bus is a Carpenter, a defunct American manufacturer that produced the classic yellow school bus. The description reads: *"El Salvador: San Salvador, fighting with the guerilla inside the city, in mexicanos area."* The second is taken from above; it shows three buses blocking a road twisting between houses with corrugated iron roofs. A small figure in green is descending from the first bus. The caption is the same; my father's unseen but he's present, somewhere behind his friend's camera three decades ago, looking at the same scene I'm seeing on my computer screen.

I write to Setboun in French, to the email address featured on the webpage: "I would like to have the chance to write to you and ask certain questions. There are things I would like to learn from you about my father, and your trips together." He answers the same day, "Yes, of course, Claude was my best friend. We had a falling out, some time ago. A long story. I haven't had any news." He then shares his contact details before concluding, "There's a book to be written about our travels."

I call him five days later, a Monday morning, via Skype. The connection crackles and swallows half his words. "Is he alive?" is the first thing Setboun asks. He's been worried by my email, thought this was the call you eventually get, "having received no news and having given non myself." "Oh, he's alive," I tell him.

He asks me how old my father is now—Setboun is the younger of the two. He quickly ventures a guess lost in the crackling. I tell him Claude is 83 then proceed to describe his life on the hill. He isn't surprised. "Yes, I know the *bonhomme*." The word evokes "man" or "guy" but also "character," as in "quite a character." I mention having seen photos of their trips and he cuts in "I even have photos of your birth." He muses for a moment on their shared experiences, saying my father came with me to Mongolia, El Salvador, the austral regions. His side of the line is deep in thought. He offers to put together some pictures of their times for me, snapshots from that world before.

"The 'artist' guy doesn't make projects. Projects are what's never carried out."
Claude Courchay

"Before." It's one of those mysteries that creep up with the onset of adulthood: who mom and dad were way back when—back "before" they were parents. That's the success of the movie *Back to the Future*, the impossible meeting with them before you came along. Sometimes it can't be as simple as asking, but I can always take his word for it. I have a time machine of sorts: I can read him…and if dad clams up, if he never opens up again, there's a lifetime of writing to piece him together.

There's that photo I've brought back from 1982, and on the right side next to the article, the dust jacket of his novel. It's hard to make out the details in black and white, but you can see a forest stretching into the title, and in a corner below, the silhouette of man's back walking on a path into the trees, rifle in hand. It's 317 pages of fiction and a sprinkling of contorted memories. That's just one of dozens of books to be found on Amazon and secondhand bookstores, and then all the fragments the Internet coughs up.

There's the cover the magazine, *Les Temps Modernes*, 27TH year, N. 291, October 1970. In red, atop the vertical listing of authors and articles, it reads Director: Jean-Paul Sartre. It's a special issue on "American Struggles," featuring articles on revolutionary black workers in Detroit, the "imperialist strategy" in Argentina, and the urban guerillas in Uruguay. Then, near the bottom: Claude Courchay – Cuba, Summer 1970.

There's an interview with French writer Catherine Rihoit, in *Simone de Beauvoir Studies*, Volume 12, 1995, under the title *A Crisis of Feminism in France?* There, amid discussions on gender politics, there's a mention in passing: "/In the summer of 1979, she was invited to accompany the up-and-coming novelist Claude Courchay to Rome."

There's a digitalized version of 25 pages of his non-fiction book, *La Soupe Chinoise*, found through the Columbia University libraries, where I get a glimpse of his childhood:

> Those mornings when joy rose above Marseille-Veyre, over the translucent wall of the hillside. The roofs of clear tiles descended unto the sea. You hurdle down stairs, down alleys. You're going

fishing. You're very small. You have the entire ocean to yourself. You fish by hand, among the bricks. The shore is full of them. It's the liberation of France and the Germans did quite a lot of dynamiting. In a couple of winters, all those bricks will turn to pink pebbles.

Finally, there's a brief review of his work, published in the French newspaper *Le Monde*, on June 24, 1978: "There is a Courchay style that pertains to a way of living and a manner of writing. Because both are in tight rapport, a rare and beautiful authenticity heightens this work where is reflected, in customs and language, our new 'lost generation.' A successful witness of our drifting world, this pure hearted vagabond has, to better see the world countercurrent, forced himself to perpetuate his own shipwreck."

The author is Jacqueline Piatier who, Wikipedia tells me, worked at *Le Monde* since 1945, and used to sign *J. Piatier* so those who didn't know her would think her a man in what was a man's world. In 1967 she founded the paper's literary supplement, which still exists today. Her account of my father seems as precise and personal as anything I've ever heard or read on Claude Courchay. She died in 2001. A "perpetual shipwreck" leaves all sorts of fragments, much as the dynamiting in Marseille by the German army turned a tide of bricks onto the shore. Someone advises me: "You pick up fragments for hours of web searches, return to your desktop, empty the bag and keep a quote, a mention in passing in someone else's interview, and extract, a review. These are the shards with which to start building the frame."

Stories need frames, and so do photographs. Framing gives focus and form, margins within which to think or observe. In framing we confine and are able to comprehend. But my father will not be confined. Someone who made it his ethos to never stand still, to never run out of stories, needs a moving frame to match blurry features. But maybe the frame doesn't have to be perfect — it just needs to capture enough of him to grasp, enough images to form a sequence. That's when I call Setboun again.

"Your habit of rushing. Life is always behind the dune. The next one. And you pass. Everything passes you by. Understand that you can stop without settling. Stick around, if you will. That's it's necessary. That…"

Claude Courchay

Michel Setboun started off as an architect, and left the routine of it for photojournalism, in the golden age of French photo agencies. In 1984, he won the World Press Photo for his work on migrant workers in Nigeria. He met my father well before that, in high school in the 1970s, when he was student and my father a teacher, in Gonesse, a suburb on the outskirts of Paris. Setboun was 17 and my father 38. "He was an iconoclast and a bit of a shit-stirrer; he put the school in disarray." Though he never had my father as his teacher, Setboun was something of a leader among students, and they met amidst the chaos. Later on, my father would be suspended for his teaching methods, despite student protest.

They kept in touch and met again years later. When Setboun started getting assignments abroad my father often went with him. "It interested him because it nourished his books." Over time, however, my father "became too much of an iconoclast" for his liking. Setboun pauses here, and adds that it's been fifteen years since they stopped talking, but that he keeps many good memories. He knew my father back in the lean years, down in *Rue Saint Jacques*, in Paris, when he had no money. Then one day he made some. But he never stopped travelling.

I ask him who my father was back then. "Someone very provoking, amusing, intelligent, outside the norm. His point of view is always interesting." Complicated, too. They often fought, and in his novels Courchay would write about him, have him play thankless roles, and even killed him off once. It came pretty close in their trip to El Salvador during the civil war, where Setboun was shot the day after my father left the country. "He always regretted that."

"When your mother came into his life I knew it wouldn't last." He says she was young and idealistic, and had all sorts of fantasies. She imagined one life and ended up with this grouchy bear. He wanted his peace and quiet, and in a way he was almost "incapacitated" when it came to those things. "His home in the 14th *arrondissement* district was really minimum service, go to the caterer, eat half for breakfast and the rest later. Spent the day reading. He has a colossal memory."

Setboun photographed my birth, and I wonder if it surprised him when he heard his 55-year-old friend was going to be a father. "Not really, all things being possible, why not that? He takes things as they come. It's not that he's indifferent, but more so if we're condemned to live, why not?"

That day an email arrives with six photographs. The first two are a series of thumbnails on a table, taken from above, with my father's figure repeated in sequences of miniature portraits. The third shows him in a t-shirt, wearing large sunglasses and raising his middle finger to the camera. In the fourth he is in the midst of drinking a beer, and his face disappears in the raised gesture, as he sits sideways on a sofa with a wooden table in front of him. He seems to intrude in the fifth; his eyes closed, amid four other men who serve as backdrop for the gesturing of a man in uniform, outlining some official truth for the ongoing conflict. In the last photograph my father is sitting on a tree trunk, in a white tee dark pants and sandals, his legs open wide and his left hand holding the wrist of his right. There are three men around him, soldiers holding their rifles. The four of them are sharing a laugh, ranging from full-throated, to wide grin, to that half smile of my father's.

What are they all laughing about, I'd like to know? That moment I decide to try calling and ask. I let the phone ring three times and hang up, then call again, and again, until I lose count. Then I think of calling a friend of his, who lives in a city a couple hours away from his hillside. We exchange small talk about her grandchildren and my life. Then she tells me he's well. Yes, the phone is working, he'd said it wasn't but it was, he just never answers. He was going a bit deaf. "If he's right next to the phone, maybe." She'd seen him on Tuesday, at the funeral of an old friend, Madame Brèneur, in a nearby town. The funeral had been full of people and my father had said, "too bad she's not here to see it."

So I called him again, and left a message this time.

Diego Courchay *is a Mexican writer who focuses on longform journalism and world literature.*

POSTSCRIPT

Tasked with choosing a significant personal image while studying abroad, I realized I had none at hand and turned to the Internet to see what it had to offer. There, after unearthing odd details and stray mentions of family members, I stumbled on a cutout of two pages from an old magazine covering an event of my father's past, for sale on eBay Italy. This came after nearly a year of trying to contact him, and failing.

Whatever questions arose from there only reached his answering machine. And yet, only a click away, a whole new facet of him started to appear, that I thought lost in the pre-digital era and the shortcomings of memory. For the first time, I found what he had written as a journalist, and what had been written about him. Granted this material, I initially resisted learning about my own father what he could tell me himself, obtaining secondhand what should arise from conversation.

Why read this transcript of his past while he's still around? Why should I be allowed to know this, and how can I deal with the fact this information had already belonged to any of his readers before me?

But maybe not having a choice was the best way to force me to search further, to discover him through his work. Not having a choice forced me to read him.

I found that there are many ways to have a conversation, many paths to each other. Talking and writing are not the same. The page has another language, a shared language and pursuit: even cut off from each other, we can meet on the page.

13 The Gangster in the Blue Serge Suit

The rise and many falls of Johnny Dio

By Ben Feibleman

Pay no attention to the man in the photo. Pay no attention to the sneer that he wears, or the balled up fist as he shoves reporters out of the way, swearing through his cigarette. Pay attention to the suit. The French-cuffs and tie pin and pocket square—the uniform of the archetypical gangster, circa 1950s, and the curtain that hides the true nature of the man behind it.

Long before Tony Soprano and the track-suit-clad Jersey mafiosos became modern icons of organized crime, the gangster wore a suit. Especially if the gangster saw himself as a businessman and an entrepreneur – the kind of man who wore a suit to work.

Dio is not coming from work. It is 1956 and he has just left a Senate committee hearing into organized crime during which he took the Fifth Amendment 140 times. He even consulted with his lawyer before giving his full name, John DioGuardi. As he left the building, he drew a cigarette and attempted to light it as he pushed through the revolving doors. The photographers were outside, waiting for him. When the scrum bumped up against him he lost the composure he'd maintained through hours of testimony and shouted, "You sons of bitches, I got a family!"

Splashed across the front pages of papers across the country, the photo of Dio's snarling face undermined the image his dark suit was meant to convey: here is a respectable man.

He had been exposed. But as what?

Before he was simply known as "Dio," he was Giovanni DioGuardi, born in 1914 in New York City. He dropped out of high school at 15. Along with his uncle, who was connected to the Lucchese crime family, Dio managed to establish a trucking union by brute force. His goal was to gain leverage over the business owners in New York City's Garment District, the city's largest industry by total employment at the time. The garment industry was reliant on the smooth delivery of product, and there already existed a union of thousands of truck drivers.

Dio had no business clout to entice drivers to participate in his racket, so he relied on threats of violence. One victim described Dio's methods in an account reported by the New York Times in 1933, in which Dio and his associates barged into the office of the trucking dispatcher, attacking him, telling him that he would be killed if his drivers did not join Dio's organization, called the "Five Boroughs Trucking Association." Numerous beatings were alleged, and while no murders at the time were attributed to Dio, drivers who refused to participate in the union would find themselves harassed with stink bombs in the cabs of their trucks and emery powder dumped in the engines, rendering them inoperable.

Gangland tactics like Dio's were different than modern methods partly because of a weak drug trade and weak legal tools for prosecution, says Kevin McCarthy, a professor at John Jay School of Criminal Justice and former chief of the Organized Crime Strike Force Division at the U.S. attorney's office in New Jersey. Mobsters were difficult to prosecute because witnesses were often afraid to testify. This changed as the successes of Special Prosecutor Thomas Dewey reached a tipping point and convinced timid witnesses that their testimony would be worth a conviction. It took four years to convict Dio on charges of coercion, conspiracy, and assault, but he pled guilty in 1937 and was sentenced to three years in Sing Sing. At the sentencing, the judge declared that Dio "suffered from a great vanity, which was quite unjustified."

In the 1930s and 40s, pleading guilty to crimes like Dio's would send you to "college" – a few years in prison that helped someone earn their underworld stripes, and then they could go back to work upon release. Like a graduate, Dio aspired for a management position. From here out, he would be the man in the suit.

"[The mafia] valued the guys they call 'earners,'" McCarthy told me. "The guys that they knew could come up with schemes." That was Dio, who saw others organizing unions and associations and added to it his own brand of thuggery.

After his release Dio moved to Allentown, Pennsylvania where he opened a dress manufacturing business. He sold it in 1950 before moving back to New York to open another dress company. If there was any doubt to Dio's motivations in labor organizing, it was exemplified in what he did after he sold the Pennsylvania business for $12,000. One year later, Dio returned, demanding another $11,200 to use his influence to prevent the plant from unionizing, while at the same time scheming with corrupt union officials back in New York to take control of his own charter, the United Auto Workers-AFL Local 102.

Dio's association with the unions brought heavy scrutiny from law enforcement which knew his reputation. This became a problem in his quest for union leadership. The parent organization accused Dio of stacking the management of local charters with unsavory characters with criminal histories, and sought a way to remove Dio and his ilk from the organization. Through the course of their investigations, they were even left baffled as to how Dio, who had never worked in the trade, acquired the charters to begin with. Union officials sought the procedural means to oust Dio, but like the challenges of Dio's criminal prosecutions, the union investigations were unable to find victims willing to testify against him.

They finally succeeded in 1954 when Dio was successfully prosecuted for tax fraud due to income he had failed to report on the sale of his Pennsylvania dress business, and the bribes made to keep the plant non-union. With his 60-day jail sentence, the union leadership finally had something they could use to justify Dio's ouster. In the end, the unions accused Dio's local organizations of not even having members, deeming them "paper locals" due to their inflated or imaginary numbers. *The Times* reported that that the New York District Attorney's office said Dio's local existed for the sole purpose of forcing "extorsive action" against the public.

Yet even with Dio's setbacks and brief jail sentence, he was still a stubborn problem for the authorities and the unions. One of the challenges to prosecuting individuals like Dio was uneven application of the law across the country as well as between city, state, and federal authorities, according to McCarthy. "It was a hodgepodge of enforcement," he said. It took time for them to evolve and catch up with the criminals. In 1956, the U.S. Attorney's office warned that New York was on the verge of a "gangster invasion."

Much like the realignment of security agencies after the 9/11 attacks, city, state, and federal law enforcement started working on ways to share evidence and communicate more efficiently to effect more successful prosecutions of organized crime.

The timing was appropriate. After Dio's release in 1954, he went right back to the labor racket he knew so well, and his methods grew even more brutal.

In April of 1956, the nationally syndicated labor columnist Victor Reisel was leaving a Manhattan radio studio. He had just finished a show during which he railed against corruption in the unions. A man, allegedly hired by Dio, approached Reisel and threw acid in his face, blinding him. But the attack backfired. The press, responding to an attack on one of their own, followed the story relentlessly. So did the FBI and the New York Police Department.

That August Dio was indicted for ordering the attack. The acid thrower was now dead of a gunshot wound to the head. The other alleged conspirators, who had fingered Dio, suddenly developed cases of amnesia. Though they ended up in prison, Dio walked. But he was hardly free.

The attack – and Dio's attempts to further infiltrate the garment business, brought him to the attention of the Senate's McClellan committee, which investigating organized crime. And it also raised the ire of one of the committee's young, aggressive attorneys, Robert F. Kennedy.

They may have gotten nothing from him that day in Washington. But the photo captured him.

He was now a public face of organized crime. The handsome suit he wore could not hide his roots as a violent thug. The feds went after him again and a year later, in 1957, Dio was convicted of extortion and conspiracy. This earned him 15 years, and though his conviction was overturned on appeal seven months into his sentence, Dio was re-arrested in New York on charges of federal tax evasion and convicted.

He was paroled in 1963. But Johnny Dio knew no profession that was not criminal in nature. He was also slipping. He started a kosher meat company called Consumers Kosher Provision which supplied products in New York City. But being a businessman is hard work, and Dio wasn't suited for it. As the company lost more and more business to a competitor, American Kosher Provisions, Dio and his associates filed for bankruptcy and he agreed to sell the company and its assets to American Kosher. Nevertheless, after an inventory had been done of all of the company's property, Dio liquidated many of the assets, from meat to machinery, thinking he could strong-arm an answer to any questions about missing items.

The plan failed, and he was sentenced to five years in prison, which he started serving in 1970 at age 56. Dio was also charged with stock fraud for, among other things, beating the original owner until the stock was sold to him at far below its true value. Although Dio beat the charge and was released from prison, within the same hour he was freed he was rearrested for a separate charge of stock fraud.

The scheme wasn't complicated: Take $300,000 in money from investors and pocket it. It was an easy case to prosecute. Like the successful-yet-overdue prosecution of Al Capone a generation before, the stolen funds were the only witness the authorities needed, and Dio was sentenced to a total of 19 years in prison.

After a lifetime of criminal work, Dio would spend his retirement behind bars. But it wasn't a typical experience in prison. Dio and other mobsters caught certain breaks—higher quality food, better accommodations and prison work assignments. Corrupt people did well in corrupt systems. In fact, in the film *Goodfellas*, as Henry Hill narrates an elaborate prison dinner routine, Johnny Dio (played by the actor Frank Pellegrino) is shown in a bathrobe, smoking a cigar as he fries a steak. He asks his fellow gangster inmate how wants it cooked.

"Medium rare, huh? An aristocrat," he says.

I n a way, it all comes back to the suit. Why the song and dance to be seen as legitimate – other than avoiding prosecution – when gangsters like Dio worked so hard to earn just enough to be middle class?

No one was living in mansions. It was a life in constant worry about the authorities, and for what? FBI files from the time show that his racket was often just nickel-and-dime payments of a few hundred or a few thousand dollars.

Johnny Dio and his family lived in a modest home, nothing to brag about. Like so many gamblers, if he'd just quit while he was ahead, he might have gotten away with it. If he'd just purchased a legitimate business with his earnings in the 1950s, before the attack on Reisel, he could have certainly done all right.

Instead he died in federal custody in Pennsylvania, hundreds of miles from home. A gangster who tried so hard to appear legitimate, who wanted to play the role of the legit entrepreneur. A man who wears a suit to work.

BEN FEIBLEMAN is a freelance journalist, a graduate of Columbia Journalism School, and a veteran of the United States Marine Corps. He lives in New York City and writes about the darkness, wherever he finds it. So far he's been to 45 countries and is still searching for the worst one.

POSTSCRIPT

Writing about Dio was tough, or rather, writing about a dead man is tough. I scoured the internet for general information and what I first came upon was excerpts from several books that fanboy'd the mafia lifestyle. They all read like they were written by men who wanted nothing more than to be Henry Hill from "Goodfellas." There weren't too many revelations there, but there were a couple comments from people who said their father was shaken down by Dio and called him a brute thug in no uncertain terms— important to know as you ingest the fire hose of historical archives. After distilling a summary of Dio's life from all that I read, I spoke to Kevin McCarthy, the former U.S. attorney who spent a career prosecuting organized crime. He helped draw the parallel between the arc of Dio's life and the arc of the Mafia's reign in the U.S.

McCarthy also helped contextualize my understanding of gangster prosecutions in history, starting with Al Capone. I had grown up in the 80s, so any reference to the Mafia was in the vein of Dick Tracy and Al Capone – caricatures when you are this many decades removed. I saw "The Untouchables" years ago and always imagined Elliot Ness, the Treasury agent who caught Capone was some brilliant man for going after him on tax evasion, but McCarthy helped explain that the legal system itself was just ill-equipped to handle this kind of crime. The kind where witnesses would back out when they were needed most. It wasn't until the 60s and 70s that there were legal tools available to help them really put these guys away for long stretches instead of "college," and that's important to understand when you are trying to figure out where all the gangsters went. (The answer: prison. It's a lot more expensive to go to "college" now, so it's hard to recruit.)

For such a notorious figure as Dio, it is easy to map out his life, but it wasn't until I read a couple hundred news clippings from the 30s and 50s that I got the details. They were a real treasure trove of witness accounts. Moreover, I suddenly understood some of the other hurdles for prosecutors; at the time it was common journalistic practice to publish the name and address of jurors in a high profile criminal trial. Of course, to me, that sounds insane, but that's how it was. The rest of the news clippings gave context that any kind of gushing tale of mafia history would skip over. There was no glamorization of the violence. Sensationalism maybe, but no one read the paper and admired these men, nor should they. It really does touch on the whole suit-wearing social armor they wore. When you peeled back the façade, they were gorillas and they were cruel.

14 The Exiles

My Family left Cuba and never stopped missing it.

By Fernanda Uriegas Fabian

I grew up in Mexico, but was raised by a Cuban family. Whenever my family got together they would talk about the time when they lived in Cuba. They would pour these stories like water into a flower pot, and I grew up as the flower.

In this photo, as in many of the old photos I sometimes find in my house in Mexico, there is a group of people, half of whom I recognize. They are my family. The other half are interchangeable friends (depending on the period in time) who would stick around my out of the ordinary family. Here they are in Varadero, the most beautiful beach in Cuba, hours away from Havana, where they lived.

The picture was taken in 1991, three days after the dissolution of the Soviet Union. The preceding years were a time of deep economic crisis in Cuba, which was losing support of the decaying Soviet Union. The country lost more than three quarters of its imports and exports, which led to shortages of food, medicine and oil. Transport and food were so scarce everyone lost weight by cycling more and eating less. "One could watch television and see how the TV hosts and artists were slowly becoming skulls," my mother's cousin told me. The government called this "the special period in time of peace." Special, because they presented it as a temporary condition, a sacrifice for the country, which had finally found peace and would soon recover.

It is hard to imagine such difficult times looking at this picture. My aunt Elsita, the woman on the left, had moved out of the country ten years earlier with her son Rainer, who she is hugging. She also has a daughter, the little girl on the right, who was born when my aunt was living in the United States. The 5-year-old was visiting her mother's country for the first time. Behind her is my mother, who had also left Cuba, to go to Mexico. You can see the joy in their faces. The only family members who are not laughing are the ones who still lived in the island: my uncle (behind Rainer's hand) and my grandmother, who hated to be photographed, caught by the camera with an uncomfortable expression. She is wearing a sailor hat I have the impression of having seen years later, in the cardboard box we kept our Halloween costumes.

I had heard the stories about the years of scarcity in Cuba through my family storytelling, but in their stories that scarcity does not seem to affect their quality of life. Instead, it forced them to get creative. Like when there were no shoes, my aunt made their own sandals using a carpet and nails she stole from under the seats in school. The only sad stories I would ever hear about Cuba were those about people who left the country, or who had died. I often wondered why then, every member of my family except my grandmother eventually decided to leave. This is the reason why this picture is important to me. It was taken at the very time the country was suffering through a crisis worse than those that had compelled them to migrate. But the very people who had left are the ones who seem happiest to be back. It was this question I had in mind as I started learning about their lives before they left Cuba.

My grandmother was three months pregnant with my mother when, in 1959 the rebels, led by Fidel Castro, ousted the US-backed dictator Fulgecio Batista. She was married to my grandfather and they were both revolutionaries. The couple had had to move houses regularly because they were afraid of being pursued by the Batista government. My grandmother, who in addition to being a doctor, loved art and painted beautifully, used to make pamphlets, drawing the hammer and sickle over Batista's head. Her older daughter, my aunt was born in 1957, four years after the revolutionary fight began. She was named Elsita, after my grandmother's first name Elsa. My mother was named Marisol, which in Spanish means sea and sun, although as a kid she insisted to be called sand and moon instead.

After the triumph of the revolution my grandfather became the head of international relations of the new government's education department. My grandmother continued to support the revolutionary forces as part of the militia. When my mother was 16 years old, she tried to join the Young Communist League. She was rejected after they learned that she had friends who played in rock bands.

With Batista's overthrow, a first wave of Cubans left for the United States. These were mainly the Cuban elite, business owners, many of whom had properties and business outside the country. Many of my family's friends left. My family stayed. Whoever left, could not come back. My grandfather used to say "No Fabian (our last name) leaves Cuba" because he saw people who left the country as *gusanos*, or traitors of the revolution.

Half a century later, my grandparents would be dead and the rest of their family far away from Cuba. When Castro died at the end of 2016, they would all celebrate.

My grandmother was a revolutionary woman. She studied medicine and became the first woman in her family to get a degree. She was also the first woman in her family to get a divorce, from my grandfather. He was a workaholic whose devotion for Communist politics bordered on the irritating. He was the sort of man who was forced to take holidays because he hadn't done it for decades. Years later, my grandmother accidentally became pregnant by someone she barely knew, a blue-eyed man everyone called Gallego (the Galician) because he was originally from Spain. At the time abortion was prohibited and doctors caught doing it could be imprisoned, but my grandmother didn't want another child. She asked a doctor friend of hers to do the procedure and offered him her car in exchange. He agreed, but as he was about to perform the procedure, he noticed a bruise on my grandmother's thigh. He backed out, afraid that the bruise might be a symptom of blood circulation problems that could complicate the abortion. As soon as she stepped out of the clinic, my grandmother felt joy. She had had a choice of rejecting or embracing her pregnancy and given the circumstances, she chose the latter.

At the time having a child without a husband was not a socially acceptable option, so she had to marry Gallego. They named the child Eugenio, after Gallego's mother. They moved together and according to my grandmother, maintained a relationship a few years before getting divorced. "I never loved him," she once told me.

My grandmother had a brother who had been working as a doctor in the United States when Castro took power, and he could never go back to Cuba. My mother remembers how her own grandmother would impatiently wait for her son's letters to arrive from across the Atlantic Ocean. She remembers how much her grandmother treasured them, putting them in a beautiful box that she kept at the top of a closet. Once, when she was a child, my mom climbed to the top of that closet, looking for that box, believing that because of the way her grandmother treated it, it must have contained a treasure. Her grandmother, she told me, eventually died of severe depression because she never got to see her son again. "I feel bad because I realize now I never saw her laughing," my mother said.

My grandmother was not yet suffering the fate of her mother. She still had her family with her —her husband Gallego, my mother, and my uncle. There was also my aunt, and in time, her son.

My aunt had wanted to be a ballerina and when she was 8 years old she was accepted into the prestigious *Escuela Nacional de Arte*, whose students danced in *Ballet Nacional de Cuba*. My aunt was one of the 16 girls from across Cuba chosen for the school that year. What my grandmother didn't know before agreeing to take her to the auditions was that the *Escuela Nacional de Arte* was a boarding school. She could not bear the thought of being away from her children, and visits were not allowed during the week. My grandmother could not deny her daughter's wishes but set one condition: my grandmother would come to the school every day after work, right before my aunt went to sleep. My aunt would come to the window and reach out her hand for my grandmother to touch. The window was too tall for them to hug, but this way my grandmother would know her daughter was fine.

It was at the school that my aunt met Roberto, a tall athletic man with blond hair who taught acrobatics and who all the girls fell for.

Roberto was 24 years old and my aunt was 14, and my mother says, considered by man to be the most beautiful woman in Havana. A romance blossomed. They were together almost two years before deciding to get married.

My grandfather's initial fury gave way to acceptance of the marriage, even though Roberto could no longer teach at the school. My aunt, however, was not expelled.

All of Roberto's family had already left for the United States. He lived by himself and my aunt believes he persuaded her to marry him because besides all the love he had for her, he didn't want to be alone in the huge house his family had left behind. Soon after my aunt turned 18, their son Rainer was born.

The relationship didn't last long. My aunt loved and admired Roberto, but her feelings towards him were those similar to the ones a sister has for his older brother. They divorced two years after they had Rainer and my aunt went back to my grandmother's house, taking her son.

My grandmother had divorced Gallego and tired of the city life, had moved to a house in the outskirts of Havana with a garden where she planted mango and guava trees. Rainer was two years old when he came to live with my grandmother, my 17 year old mother and my uncle, who was 11. It was as if Rainer had three mothers to spoil him and a brother to play with.

The house was always full of people. My mother was a blossoming extroverted teenager who made friends almost every day. Many came to see my ingenious grandmother as well, a doctor and single mother who everyone in the neighborhood respected. My grandmother would cook for them, and they would play music.

My aunt never pursued a dancing career. She decided she wanted to study architecture, but she did not get a place because it was reserved for the children of the military. The family, like so many others, was feeling the repressive ways of the government that rewarded loyalty to the party and punished dissenters and critics. My aunt agreed with some aspects of the system and disagreed with others, but felt like she could not share her opinion.

"We had the basic things with that system, things were alright, but it is human nature to want more and if you wanted more you had to get into the system," she said. "You had to have two faces. You were either intensely revolutionary to gain access or you had to act hypocritically."

The Committees for the Defense of the Revolution were in every neighborhood and monitored what people said. If you criticized the government in the least, you could be accused of having 'ideological problems', as they called them. Some were even imprisoned. My mother and aunt couldn't even share their opinions with their father without causing a fight, and they both believe their relationship was hurt because he was such a fanatic. Even now my mother is wary of criticizing the Cuban government, even when she is talking from Mexico. Through it all it would be a long time before anyone in my family left because they all knew that they could not come back.

My aunt did not want to leave forever and yet did not like the ideological repression and saw few opportunities for her in the country. She knew that if she married a foreigner, she could get a permit to go in and out of the country. The first time she met my uncle, a Mexican diplomat working in Cuba at the time, she was sweeping the terrace of the house. His name was also Roberto, but he was very different from her ex-husband. He was a short and not particularly attractive man, but she found him very intelligent and well positioned. She agreed to go out with him. They ended up marrying.

Roberto was transferred back to Mexico, which meant my aunt and Rainer would go with him. It was 1982 and Rainer was 9 years old. He had spent seven years living in my grandmother's house, and the family could not imagine life without him. My mother clearly remembers the small squared shirt and blue jeans Rainer was wearing the day he left. After they said goodbye, my mother and grandmother sat on the couch silently for several minutes. "It was one of the saddest moments of my life" my mother said.

My mother eventually migrated to Mexico as well. She got a visa to visit my aunt and in one of those trips, she met my father, married and decided to move. She tried to convince my grandmother to move as well, but she refused.

My aunt and my mother did come back to Cuba every few months to visit. And it was on and in one of those trips they decided to go to the beach in Varadero, where the picture that led me to write this story was taken.

"My greatest excitement was to go back to my country," my aunt told me. "But every time I went I saw it worse and worse." At the very moment when the picture was taken, you can see the excitement she talks about on her face. Rainer was back in Cuba, living with my grandmother because he did not like Mexico and missed his home country. My aunt was visiting his son in the place where he raised him, remembering that time he lived with her siblings and mother.

The picture represents a wonderful moment for my family – a reunion. But there are few things worth remembering from that trip. They were having such a good time that they wanted to stay for longer than planned, but the rooms at the hotel were full. Nestor, my mother's boyfriend at the time (who is all the way to the right in the picture) managed to convince a local family to let them stay at their house. They agreed, and my uncle didn't pay only with money, he also paid them with four chickens and two bottles of cooking oil.

They had a fun trip, but the deterioration of the country could not be hidden and made my aunt extremely sad and melancholic. On the plain returning from that trip, Elsita promised herself she would not go back until Fidel Castro died. She almost kept that promise because she went back 25 years after, only two months before that happened.

During all those years, my grandmother never wanted to leave her country, even though all of her children had left. I remember going to the supermarket in Mexico as a child to buy blanks for her shotgun, because you could not find them in Cuba. My grandmother needed them so she could fire away whenever she heard someone around the house. But thieves still broke in and stole paintings and furniture while she slept. Her children paid someone to take care of her, but caregivers were unreliable and stole from her as well.

When I was 11 years old, I flew from Mexico with my dad to visit my grandmother. He dropped me off at her house and went to Islas Caimanes, an island near by, to attend to some business, or now that I think about it, maybe to meet a Cuban lover. I ended up staying with my grandmother for a week. It was ten years after she started to live by herself. I didn't know her well because I visited Cuba only every few years. By this time her health, both physical and mental, was deteriorating. I remember she couldn't cook, and when she did, I felt truly sad and worried about my health with every bite I ate to please her.

I remember once we stole a little chick from the neighbor (who had so many he would never realize we did). We didn't take care of it and it died. My grandmother, keeping his death a secret, hid it in a kitchen drawer. I found it as I was looking for scissors.

I remember that even though there were many beds in the house and we could have slept in separate rooms, she slept on the floor next to me so we wouldn't be apart. She let me sleep on her bed, which was not that comfortable. Most beds in Cuba are old. Even now, there are still people who work repairing mattresses.

Every night before going to bed we would spend some time with the lights off, talking about life. I remember how one night she said "I am going to tell you something but you have to promise you won't tell anyone. It is a secret." She confessed she had not intended to have my uncle or to marry Gallego. She told me the whole story with the honesty of life long friends. Amazed, I asked if my mom knew. No, she said, "You, Gallego and myself are the only people in the world who know about this." Only later did I learn that everyone in the family already knew this. I was pleased she wanted to take me into her confidence. I considered that "secret" like a gift, an act of trust that made me feel, maybe for the first time, like someone worth enough to be trusted.

Eventually my grandmother did leave Cuba. We had to bring her to Mexico because she could not live by herself anymore, but she hated it. By this time I was studying abroad and I barely saw her, but the woman they brought to the house was not the grandmother I got to know on my trip as an 11-year-old. She had dementia and barely knew who we were. When my grandmother died three years ago, I remember my mother feeling guilty, telling me she got sick so fast because she was lonely for so many years in Cuba.

When I see this picture in Varadero, as much as when I go to Havana and see my deceased grandmother's deteriorating house, I think of a time I only lived through my family's storytelling. I picture my family spending time together at the terrace. I mentally fix the cracks in the mirrors and the water leakage on the roof.

When my mother visited Cuba for the first time after my grandmother died, she would desperately clean, set rat traps, spray insecticide, water the plants. I would help her, scrubbing the bathtub, washing every clothing item in the house and sweating like crazy during the Caribbean summer. We would exhaust ourselves, trying to bring the house back to the way it was so long ago, before everyone left.

Exhausted, we would finally sit at the terrace to drink espresso ("one must always drink coffee sitting down" my grandma and my mother would always say). My mother would rock back and forth in the rocking chair, realizing as much as I did that there was no way we could fix the enormous house, as much as there was no way we could go back in time, when the house was full of life, the time the picture evokes.

"I miss my mom so much," she would tell me as tears would peacefully go down her cheeks.

- - -

FERNANDA URIEGAS is a Mexican and Cuban journalism student at Columbia University who has lived in India, the Netherlands, Canada and the United States. She has a bachelor in the social sciences and specializes in social justice long-form writing. You can find some of her work at https://medium.com/@fernanda.uriegas.fabian

Purpose

My parents had dreams for me. They weren't mine.

By Sweenie Saint-Vil

This is what I remember: I remember graduating from college and helping my parents pack their van with all my possessions. I remember saying goodbye as they drove off and I remember how that night I went to a friend's house and how we had mac and cheese for dinner and Red Lobster biscuits and wine. I remember how we found the Hoya theme song we had written in freshman year and tried to rap it. We watched the episode of Scandal we'd missed. I remember walking back to my dorm with a friend and how I went to her room and watched her pack. We had gone to high school together and I thanked her for helping me get through four years at Georgetown. The last thing I remember was taking a picture of my room.

I remember nothing about the next day. This had nothing to do with drinking or drugs – I was a straight arrow. I do not remember how I got to Union Station. I do not remember buying the bus ticket. I do not remember whether my friend from high school took the bus back with me. I remember nothing about the four and a half hour ride to New York, or the hour subway ride from Penn Station, or was it Port Authority? My mother may have met me in Manhattan, but I don't remember.

My grandmother was waiting at my parents' home to see me. We spoke, I think, for about an hour before I made my excuses, went upstairs and closed the door to my bedroom where I would spend most of the coming months, privately sulking in my misery.

I have two brothers. One gave me $200. The other Mack, did not know, and nor did I, that his gift would come later that summer, in a form I could have never anticipated.
Things were expected of me. And I delivered.

I started reading when I was three. I used to wake my father up on weekends so he could help me pronounce the words that were too challenging for me to sound out. He never complained because he liked the ambition, my determination to learn, something that would serve me well for most of my years in school.
I stood out when I got to pre-school. From what my parents tell me, I surprised teachers because I used big words and could already write my name. In kindergarten, the teachers were impressed with how fluently I spoke Creole, a skill I picked up from my grandmother, and relied on me to translate for a student who had just moved from Haiti and could hardly understand English. That's the thing about being smart; people start to depend on you.

We had an assignment later that year about what we wanted to be when we grew up. I said I wanted to be a nurse like my mother and my parents clapped and praised my decision. It was almost as if I won American Idol, the way they were so excited. Now they knew and fully supported what I was working towards.

I was the one who wrote on the board when the teachers were too lazy to do it themselves, the one who would volunteer to read when the teacher's requests for readers were met with silence, the "student of the month," the one who almost always had a perfect score on exams. I graduated at the top of the class and received a full scholarship to Bishop Loughlin, a college preparatory school in Brooklyn.
Things changed little in high school. I was first in my grade on the Honor Roll but I never spoke about my grades. I didn't speak much in class anymore. My spots on the cheerleading and step teams

allowed me to be a "cool nerd." I was valedictorian again and after graduation was heading to Washington, DC for college.

I didn't know what I was getting into when I applied to Georgetown. I didn't think I was going to get in. I didn't involve my parents in the process. I didn't think they'd want me to go away and away was where I wanted to be: away from being "perfect," away from the pressure that built up every time I got an A, away from being expected to become a doctor -- an evolution of my kindergarten dream of being nurse –a dream that was more their dream than mine.

I'm a daughter of Haitian immigrants who came here speaking little English. My mother worked in a hospital and my father worked for the city housing authority. They raised us – my two brothers and me – to have careers that paid us well. My mother saw opportunity as a nurse, and perhaps even a doctor. I didn't want to disappoint them.

But school was no longer easy at Georgetown. Even though I lived far from home I could not escape the pressure of my parents' expectations. If anything, it got worse. For the first time I was away from Brooklyn, away from my family. I was no longer in school surrounded by people of color. I stood out as a black woman and experienced racism for the first time. Classes were hard and I wasn't a star student. It was the first time I could explore life and my studies without parental restrictions. It was where I'd realize that living by the book, my parents' book, was draining, especially when it was completely different than the book I would have written.

I got my first dose of racism on move in day. I'd left my government ID back home in Brooklyn and was told I couldn't get my school ID without it. I'd need it to get access to buildings, meal plans, and printing so I pulled my high school ID out to verify my identity. The lady behind the desk said traveling back to New York was my best bet. But just minutes before, she had let the white boy in the same situation sign into his account to confirm it was actually him. My father noticed it and yelled, and I got my ID. My father was used to this. He could fight his way out. It was new to me. I was taken aback.

I moved in and got ready to participate in Welcome Week. I was still high off being valedictorian and would make sure I used that in my introduction. I'd soon find out that I was one of many who'd accomplished this feat, except I'd achieved far less than the others had. They were fluent in several languages, had traveled or studied abroad, took years of AP courses, and already had years of experience in their desired fields. All I had to my name was that I was valedictorian and that meant nothing to them.

My 18th birthday was two days later. My parents had already gone home. I knew nothing about the area and I hadn't yet made any new friends. My high school friend took me to the nearest restaurant for some wings but our time was limited...we had to return to our orientation group in the next few hours. I thought about how much more fun my birthday would have been back home.. I'd waited all my life to turn 18 but I was on my own. Classes started. There were very few black students – only one or two in the smaller sections. The other black kids were not the least bit intimidated. Everyone would form groups and talk before class began. I would pretend to text on my phone. I had met many of the students during orientation so I hated having to introduce myself again; it was only a reminder that I sucked in comparison to my peers.

I was a pre-med student studying healthcare management and had a set curriculum for the next four years. I didn't have the luxury of exploring different electives before declaring a major at the end of sophomore year. I had biology and chemistry my first semester. One alone was hard. Taking two was death. I barely passed my biology class. And chemistry was worse, especially when we were split into groups. I never before understood how it felt to be the last person chosen. I knew they didn't want me, a black girl, in their group. I felt ignored and not respected. I failed the first exam and barely passed the second. The professor told me that I was wasting my time and should drop the class because I had no chances of passing. I withdrew that afternoon and told my parents.

My father said that he was disappointed that I'd given up. Still, he and my mother said it was okay when I cried and said I felt like a failure.

I forced myself to go to classes in the second semester. I found comfort in listening to R&B music and Skyping my family and friends. I also slept a lot -- between my classes, before I did my homework, after I did my homework.

I thought of transferring. I did some research on Howard and St. John's and a few other schools searching for one good enough to convince my parents. But I knew that unless I chose to attend an Ivy League, there was no way out of Georgetown. My parents wouldn't allow that.

I went home as often as I could which helped because I didn't often call, even though my mother left me voice messages reminding me to call her. It was not that I didn't want to call her; I didn't want to burden her with my complaints. My father, sensing my unhappiness and not wanting to add to the stress, didn't ask to see my grades at the end of the semester. Still, that summer, my family made a point of all the weight I had gained.

I was no happier in my sophomore year. I felt ever more alone, even when I had a boyfriend who I now see was a bandage, a temporary fix on my feeling so badly about myself. Although my grades improved, I had checked out. I cannot remember what I learned.

One of my professors, sensing something was wrong, approached me after I'd missed two classes and suggested that I get evaluated for issues related to stress. The woman I met with always had some chocolate to share with me. She thought I was cool. I liked her sweaters and she liked my shoes. She always offered a compliment. She advised me to seek counseling, but I was not so sure. My mother always cautioned me about seeking psychological help. People who get this help are usually crazy, she said. Go if you want to be labeled crazy. So I went.

I only went to three sessions. The psychologist asked if I wanted antidepressants and I declined. Still, it was good to talk. Counseling, however, came with a fee and I was on my mother's insurance plan and so I knew she'd be informed if I made any visits to a doctor.

My father still wanted to see my grades, which were mixed. Friends were doing better than I was. I tried to avoid showing him my grades but couldn't run once he did ask to see them. I was used to him punishing me when he was upset with me but he simply said he was disappointed in me. That felt much worse. In my senior year my grades improved and I was happier. But then, at a jobs fair, I met with a recruiter for a healthcare organization who saw right through me. He pulled me aside and told me that he wasn't convinced I wanted to work in the field. I went home and cried even though I had finally gotten what I needed: the confirmation that I was preparing for the wrong career. I just didn't know how obvious it was to other people. Obvious to others, except my parents.

Facebook was the devil post graduation. I would scroll down my newsfeed to see posts about friends accepting job offers to Deloitte, Goldman Sachs, Morgan Stanley. I saw acceptances to Columbia's Business School, University of Pennsylvania, Fordham University's Law School. Everyone had it all figured out, except me.

I applied for jobs every day through LinkedIn, Indeed, Careerbuilder, and Simplyhired. But I was making things harder for myself. I applied not for healthcare jobs but for positions at Viacom, Universal Music Group, Atlantic Records, and Time Inc. I got rejection after rejection.

I binged on chocolate, cookies, any homemade meal...I slept a lot. I would be up from 11 at night til 4 or 5 in the morning watching television and comparing my life to everyone else's. I barely stepped foot outside. I stayed in my room and hid from my father. I knew our next conversation was going to be about my next step in life.

My mother begged me to speak with him so I did. It went badly. He blamed me for being lazy since I couldn't land a job. He told me he hadn't paid my tuition for me to stay at home all day. I cried to my mother, asking her why he would think I thought being unemployed was okay after I'd worked so hard to graduate, that as far as he knew, graduating came easy to me. She said his intentions were good, and that she felt the same way he did. My dad would later bring up graduate school. "I hope you don't think a bachelor's degree is enough," he said. "It means nothing. Everyone has one."

And then, in the midst of my despair over feeling like a failure to myself, and to my parents, came unexpected gift: a distraction. My brother's girlfriend was pregnant. I finally felt that I had reason to leave the house, if just to see her and touch her belly. There was a baby shower to arrange and that day I helped wrap the utensils in white napkins. I helped come up with his middle name. I counted down the days. It was as if a new narrative, a new story, had begun to unfold in my life. It was more than a distraction, because I had seen how distractions did not work. This was exciting and fun and there was so much to anticipate.

I was at a wedding the day my nephew was born. I had found work at the Italian American Civil Rights League, a non-profit organization. I told everyone at work. I couldn't keep the news to myself. I took the bus and the subway to the city, to the Manhattan hospital where I thought the baby was born. The secretary at the desk said there was no one staying at the hospital by my "sister" Soleil's name. I called her and I discovered I had to go to the hospital's Brooklyn affiliate.

I watched my nephew Carter sleeping. Soleil asked why I hadn't held him and then she placed him in my arms. I could not stop crying.

Soliel took Carter and asked me what was wrong. It was the first time anyone had asked in months. I began to explain.

- - -

SWEENIE SAINT-VIL is a writer with a passion for pop culture and humanizing celebrities. Follow her on social media for updates on new posts.

ABOUT THE AUTHORS

We are a collection of writers and journalists from all walks of life. But our paths all led to Columbia Journalism School. You can find more information on each writer at medium.com/@memory-project. We hope you enjoyed our memories and would love to hear from you.

www.ingramcontent.com/pod-product-compliance
Lightning Source LLC
Chambersburg PA
CBHW061725020426
42331CB00006B/1104